Herman Windolf

And the Queensland German Baptists

Edited by Edgar (Ted) Stubbersfield

DEDICATION

This book is dedicated to Windolf Family at Tent Hill Baptist Church who have now become my family in Christ.

CONTENTS

CONTENTS

ACKNOWLEDGMENTS

Rebekka Geitner, Historian, BallinStadt Emigration Museum, Hamburg, Germany. She was a willing and helpful source of information.

David Parker of Baptist Heritage Queensland for permission to reproduce material copyright to them and for extra information and images.

Selwyn Windolf, for introducing me to the writings of Herman Windolf and for trusting me with valued family records.

INTRODUCTION

Half the members of my church, the Tent Hill Baptist Church, are descended from or married to descendants of Herman Windolf. Herman was the first ordained German Baptist pastor to come to Queensland and ministered initially among the German Baptists in the Fassifern Scrub area (modern Kalbar). Perhaps half our church is a little exaggeration but what is not exaggerated the godly shadow he cast over five following generations.

I was introduced to Herman when I preached a sermon on revival when his name came up in association with local but long forgotten movements of God's Spirit. One of our members, Selwyn Windolf handed me documents prepared many years ago by Glenn Roberts which included translations of reports Herman sent home to Germany for publication in Christian magazines. They covered his journey through Hamburg to Brisbane and the journey to Fassifern Scrub and the start of his ministry. They were fascinating reading and I believed others would enjoy reading them also, hence this book.

It was a different time and a different world when men seemed to have greater strength, endurance and resolve. Without this they could not have turned the "howling wilderness" into some of the finest farmland in Australia. This small book allows us a window into this generation whose faith was tried in adversity and tempered by the vision of a better life that could come to them and their generations.

Some of the material in this book is copyright to the Queensland Baptist Historical Society and is used with their permission. I have not been able to contact Glenn Roberts who also wrote some of the material but it appears to be in public domain.

1. FROM GERMANY TO QUEENSLAND, AUSTRALIA

The voyage of Brother H. WINDOLF as published in the German Baptist magazine "Der Pilgor" - (The Pilgrim) in the year 1878 P. 6ff

1. FROM HOME TO HAMBURG.

The beloved king had spoken and His order was clear and precise. Once before His voice had called on Abraham to leave fatherland and friends behind to travel to a far away and foreign land selected for him by Jehovah

Now, His inscrutable will had ordered the poorest of His messengers to follow the Macedonian call of dear brothers in faith in far away Australia. After long years of prayers and hope their supplications were granted by the mighty king of Zion. My soul was filled with grateful and humble admiration for the providence of the Lord and therefore my decision was an easy one. In fact, I personally had no choice - the Lord Himself had decided and I simply obeyed the orders received. I pray to the Lord that the grace of Christ will be with me to fulfil the task entrusted to me.

The day of departure arrived after completion of a multitude of preparations but - marching orders were received and so we went.

Braunschweig c. 1880

To part from all our beloved in Braunschweig (Brunswick)[1] was not easy. All the joys and sorrows of the past at home will forever be remembered. Other leave takings were still to come.

On the 30th of September 1877, we[2] departed from Braunschweig on the first train and arrived at noon in Einbeok where we interrupted the journey to pay a last visit to my beloved mother, brothers and sisters. To our regret we could stay for a very short time only as I had promised our community in Holmstedt and vicinity to devote a Sunday to them. Our hearts more heavy as this parting was the hardest one, but the sweet hope to meet again one day alleviated our grieving

---

[1] Then capital of the state of Brunswick until it was disestablished in 1946.
[2] He and his wife, both aged 31, and two children Frederick (3) and Hannah (1).

We left Einbeck at midday on the 1st of October. Here I was born and had grown up in the womb of the community receiving invaluable blessings over the years. Destination of the day was the sugar factory Freudelbusch near Helmstedt, residence of the parents of my beloved wife. Her father - T. Fluegge Sen, is the taxation official at the factory (Translators remark: apparently the equivalent to nowadays accountant).

On the 2nd of October, the day of the Lord, we walked, accompanied by my in-laws to Suepplingon, a neighbouring village where the large prayer house of the community is situated. I was favoured to address the community with a parting sermon. The text of the morning was the 121st Psalm and for my afternoon service I selected Philippians 2, 5-10. May the word of the Lord bear fruit.

The moment of the final parting approached much too fast; however, it had to be and we took our leave in the hope of a happy reunion at the throne of the lamb.

Accompanied by many blessings, prayers and memories we departed in the early morning hours of the 5th October by train and arrived in the evening of the same day in lovely Hamburg, the starting point of our voyage. An unexpected and happy surprise was waiting for us passing through the Braunschweig railway station. Many friends had assembled there to see us off once more. God bless you, friends, for your moving love.

MEYER & CO.

Zum großen Auswanderer-Hause.

Hamburg, Theerhof Nº 5—8,

unmittelbar an sämmtlichen Bahnhöfen und in der Nähe des Hafens.

Preise für Logis und Kost per Tag:
I. Classe ℳ 3. II. Classe ℳ 2. III. Classe ℳ 1.50 ₰

Lager von Matratzen, Decken, Blechgeschirren,

Getränken etc. Geldwechsel-Geschäft.

Diese Karte ist bei Ankunft in Hamburg sichtbar zu tragen, damit unsere Angestellten die Passagiere sogleich in Empfang nehmen können.

Advertisement for Emigration House

Wrapped in deep thoughts of the Lord's grace, clinging to the rock of faith, we arrived at Hamburg after uneventful hours of train travelling.

Accommodation was reserved for us in the large "Emigration House", Hamburg - Theerhof No. 5-8.[3] First thing next morning we hurried to meet my uncle brother H. Windolf Sen., who worked for many years as a stalwart missionary of the sailors mission throughout the harbour.[4] He was not at home in pursuit of his daily work but his dear wife made us welcome and feel at home and the hours of waiting for his return passed quickly. He came home late in the evening and again time flew exchanging mutual experiences and family stories. We returned to our quarters late at night and the next day

---

[3] An even larger emigration house, said to be the largest boarding house in the world was run by the HAPAG shipping company. "Many thousands of people from all over Europe arrived here every week to await the departure of their ship. For approximately five million people, between 1850 and 1934, Hamburg was the gateway to a new life".

[4] Herman's uncle, also called Herman, was supported by Spurgeon's church, the Metropolitan Tabernacle. His labours can be read in the Sword and Trowel June 1865. http://www.godrules.net/library/spurgeon/NEW9spurgeon_a9.htm Date accessed 22 October 2014.

was devoted to a much needed period of rest. However, in the evening we went out in company of some other relatives to see some sights of the city.

Johann Gerhard Oncken[5] – The father of the German Baptists

In the early hours of next morning – 7th October - I set out to formally report to the Senior of the German Baptist Mission - brother Oncken, He just had commenced the morning family service at my arrival. It was an experience to listen to his sermon - Joh. 7, 38. The "Old Man" of the faith is well preserved in body and soul but - to my regret - I noticed that his memories of the outside world were faltering. With his well known, warm interest, the dear brother listened to my report about my Australian vocation. His advice, relevant hints and encouragement will be treasured in my memory. Deeply moved, I took my leave. May this meeting be a constant remainder to persist in faith with the work of the Lord.

2. EMBARCATION AND VOYAGE TO ENGLAND – OUR STAY IN LONDON

---

[5] It is reported that "during his ministry as a Baptist preacher, J. G. Oncken constituted over 280 Baptist churches and 1222 preaching stations. He founded over 170 churches in Scandinavia and the Slavic states. He also formed 771 Sunday Schools in Germany" Wikipedia date accessed September 20, 2014.

№ 501 a

Verzeichniss

der Personen, welche zur Auswanderung nach *Australien* via *London* durch Unterzeichnete engagirt sind und mit dem Dampfschiffe *Martin* Capitän *Goslin* unter *englischer* Flagge zunächst nach *London* befördert werden.

Abgang des Schiffes, d. *7 October* 187*7*

509 a

N.	Zuname.	Vorname.	Geschlecht männlich	Geschlecht weiblich	Alter.	Bisheriger Wohnort.	Im Staate oder in der Provinz.	Bisheriger Stand oder Beruf.	Ziel der Auswanderung, Ort und Land	Zahl der Personen	Erwachsene und Kinder über 10 Jahr	Kinder unter 10 Jahr	unter 1 Jahr
1	2		3		4	5	6	7	8	9	10	11	12
1	Alexius	Michael	1		3	Essen	Rheinprovinz	Landm.	Brisbane in Queensland		1		
2	Schultz	Heinrich	1		23	do	do	do	do		1		
3	Regling	Friedrich	1		25	Wollnow	Uckermark	do	do		1		
4	do	Henriette		1	24	do	do	frau	do		1		
5	do	Anna		1	3	do	do	Kind	do			1	
6	do	Bergine		1	1	do	do	do	do			1	
7	Neumann	Ludwig	1		17	Eickel	Westfalen	Landm.	do		1		
8	Balzas	Onyas	1		24	Essen	Rheinprovinz	do	do		1		
9	Szandezak	Friedrich	1		33	Aachen	Preussen	do	do		1		
10	Anbeka	Ludwig	1		45	Danzig	do	do	do		1		
11	do	Emilie		1	32	do	do	frau	do		1		
12	do	Martha		1	14	do	do	Kind	do		1		
13	do	Paul	1		7	do	do	do	do			1	
14	do	Amanda		1	4	do	do	do	do			1	
15	do	Alwine		1	1	do	do	do	do			1	
16	Windolf	Friedrich	1		31	Braunschweig	Braunschweig	Landm.	do		1		
17	do	Elise		1	31	do	do	frau	do		1		
18	do	Friedrich	1		8	do	do	Sohn	do			1	
19	do	Hanne		1	2	do	do	Tochter	do			1	
20	Michel	Carl	1		36	Essen	Rheinprovinz	Landm.	do		1		
21	Aurow	Wilhelm	1		47	Wollnow	Uckermark	do	do		1		
22	do	Friederike		1	48	do	do	frau	do		1		
23	do	Wilhelmine		1	15	do	do	Tochter	do		1		
24	do	Elisabeth		1	13	do	do	do	do		1		
25	do	Friedrich	1		4	do	do	Sohn	do			1	
26	Prokurier	Wilhelm	1		27	Schmölln		Landm.	do		1		
27	do	Caroline		1	29	do	do	frau	do		1		
28	do	Wilhelm	1		10	do	do	Sohn	do		1		
29	do	Carl	1		3	do	do	do	do	29	20	7	

Wir erklären hiedurch an Eides Statt, dass die vorstehenden Angaben nach unserm besten Wissen richtig sind, dass auch soviel uns bekannt, unter den in diesem Verzeichnisse aufgeführten Personen sich keine befinden, deren Beförderung verboten ist und dass wir mit dem oben genannten Schiffe auch solche Personen wissentlich nicht befördern wollen.

HAMBURG, d. *9 October* 187*7*

Unterschrift des Expedienten

Passenger List for Windolf Embarkation

Late in the afternoon of the same day (7th Oct.) we boarded a coach to be transported with all our baggage to the pier. A party of young people had left in advance to walk down but had got lost on the way, The search for them delayed the arrival of our party at the jetty for more than one hour. The unloading and transfer of crates, chests and chattels to the ship were completed at a late hour after strenuous and time consuming effort: (We had to carry and stow): after all this we were ready now to find our own accommodation aboard to bed down out weary bones.[6]

Embarkation from Hamburg c. 1875

Accommodation allocated to us was finally found in a space called 'the second cabin" Entering the low and narrow compartment, the first encompassing glance was not exactly inviting. The room was crammed to capacity with humanity clad in a variety of folk

---

[6] The route to Australia via London was the low cost fare. Geitner, Rebekka. *Pers. Com.* 1 October 2014.

costumes and we finally found a small space to sit on the floor after much effort to penetrate the milling crowd. The vast majority of the emigrants had been aboard for many hours and many had been continuously on the grog since last night. The whole room was choking with clouds of tobacco smoke. If we would have had our choice, we might have turned on our heels at the threshold in view of the repulsive fug and smoke and the false cheerfulness of the crowd. With the Lord's assistance we managed to carry on.

Hamburg Harbour 1875

There was no hope of any sleep. Approximately half of us - mainly married couples with children - found places in the small and narrow berths, one above the other, and all others - mostly single men - had to make do with a space on the floor, which created much discontent. Aroused by the bottle they squabbled and fought all and the racket continued all night.

After midnight the anchor was weighed, the ships machine turned over slowly and we had a last view of Hamburg's passing sea of lights. "Farewell oh beloved German homeland" may well have been the thought of many. Now we are steaming steadily and quiet downriver in direction of the mouth of the Elbe River. In the morning - the first Sunday of the voyage - which was not destined to be a day of rest after all, we saw only a small strip of land far away on the horizon and soon, the last visible remainder of the fatherland had disappeared too. Noisy quarrels started again and continued throughout the Sabbath. The bottle went around again, cards were played and the air was full of swearing and dirty songs. Our hearts were heavy to hear and see such godless behaviour on the day of the Lord but we found some consolation in the quiet reading of God's word. In the afternoon we tried to talk to some of the quiet and serious people and distributed pamphlets.

Already in the morning flocks of storm-birds had been sighted and soon after midday the waves started to mount and as soon as we entered the open North Sea the storm hit us with full force - for us a complete novel and frightening experience. A damp mist lays above the water and we are surrounded by high and turbulent waves. Like a secret force ascending from the great deep, wave after wave towers above us, breaks and is followed by others in endless succession. The combs are covered with white foam in sharp contrast to the dark green colours of the waves. Howling gusts of wind shriek through the rigging and blocks and tackle crash against masts and broadsides. The ship is tossed to and fro like a nutshell and groans and moans in joints and seams. Until now many passengers had been on deck attracted by the exalted majesty of the sea. Suddenly a tremendous wave washed over the deck compelling everybody to flee into the protection of the cabins.

The cabin was a picture of utmost misery getting worse from minute to minute. Nearly everyone of the travellers fell victim to the dreaded seasickness. Wave after wave now rolled continuously over the ship and the situation deteriorated rapidly. Agonizing retching and painful vomiting of partly digested food and quantities of green slime penetrated the cabin with a repulsive, sour stink. The second stage of the sickness soon followed: headaches, dizziness and deadly weakness and numbness of limbs and body. One can imagine the effect this all had on a crowd of humanity crammed into the small space and it is not surprising that finally even the strongest constitutions succumbed. From all passengers only two - at the most three - were spared. No pen can describe the scenes we saw, and the most vivid imagination is unable to paint a true picture. The fury of the storm was still increasing and it seemed that the ship - at any moment - would be drawn into the abyss or smashed against cliffs. The screams and howls could be heard above the noise of storm and waves, although most of the victims are now stretched out prone and helpless with empty heads and stomachs, unable to move limbs and body and apathetic and indifferent to fate. The ship is a helpless plaything of the furious elements.

Cheer up Christians - you need not have to fear - is not the saviour aboard with you, the ruler of storms and waves....?! Yes - indeed - we felt safe and happy in the knowledge to have the right helmsman aboard and no matter how much the elements raged, we felt as safe and sheltered in the presence of the Lord as if we were in the strongest castle! Where was now the foolish cheerfulness of the children of this world? Their faces white, the eyes dead and expressionless and filled with fear and insolent, blaspheming mouths open only to scream in fear! Oh, what a sorry and pitiable picture.

During the height of the storm we sang hymns of Jesus and some Catholics sang and prayed aloud to Jesus, Maria and Joseph and all Saints,

Later on we heard that our confession and fearless attitude in the hours of deadly danger had earned us the respect of the mockers and had created confidence and trust in many other souls.

After midnight the vehemence of the storm diminished and the light of the rising dawn showed that the waves already had considerably subsided. Gradually the sea quietened more and more. Later during the day the coastline appeared on the horizon and in the afternoon we entered the mouth of the River Thames. The closer we came to the City of London the more ships were met and sighted. Shortly we passed the many magnificent shipyards and factories which line the shore in fabulous sizes and numbers. The closer we came to this modern Babel, the more we were impressed.

At 7 o'clock in the evening the ship anchored in the vicinity of the Tower Bridge near the famous Tower of London. A ferry transferred us and our luggage to the Quay, Everybody was happy to feel land underfoot again but our general situation was not enviable. Tired and hungry as we were, we were enclosed by the throng of a milling crowd and had to guard our baggage which was stacked on the landing.

After more than 1 ½ hours an old Jew approached us in the German language and professed to be some sort of an agent. He arranged for the transport of our luggage by a horse drawn cart to a German boarding house. All people, including children, had to walk. We arrived at 11 o'clock and were finally penned up in our quarters in Dearling Street (Darling Road or Row?). This was a narrow den much too small for our numbers. Most of us had to sleep on the bare floor in company of rats, mice and certain other smaller vermin. The food was un-appetizing and hardly edible but the German hosts assured that they did the utmost possible for us. Well - they certainly understood their "business" - the number of people in our party represented a fair amount of profit for then.

This became even more obvious when the mentioned Jew presented our bill on the next day. Per head we had to pay 3 harks for the transport of luggage, regardless of quantity, and further 6 harks per person for two days board and lodgings (although we had meals on one day only). This in spite of the written confirmation in our pocket -issued by the Hamburg agent - that transportation of luggage and persons as well as board and lodging in London, were included in the passage money we had previously paid in Hamburg.

In the afternoon I had the opportunity to see in company with other members of our party some of the sights in London. After walking close to the business centre, we boarded a horse drawn tram and drove through the streets of the merchant palaces past St. Paul's Cathedral, the Tower, the Waterloo monument and other sights and returned by boat on the River Thames to our lodgings.

III. ON THE RIVER THAMES, EVENTS IN THE CHANNEL,

West India Dock

Late afternoon on the 10th October we were transported with our goods and chattels to the West India Docks where our ship the "Gauntlet" was anchored - a three master of 667 tons. This ship is far more roomy and comfortable than the "Martin" and is a palace by comparison. The steerage deck is divided by partitioning walls into three separate rooms, one for families with children under fourteen years of age and their parents and the other two are for single people, one for males and the other one for females. The family room in which we were accommodated, had on either side long rows of bunks, each approximately 4-5 ft. wide and 6-7 ft. long - one above and one underneath the other. At the distribution by lots, I drew the last number which - to my delight - consisted of two berths for my wife, two children and myself. The upper bunk was lighted by a small bullseye and served as a "reading room" at daytime and as a bed at night. Much more comfort can be found in such a limited space as many people may be able to imagine.

At night, a tug towed us to Gravesend, an important and sheltered anchorage for seagoing ships. The "Gauntlet" had to anchor here in order to replenish provisions and equipment. Some other necessary work had to be carried out in order to prepare the ship for the storms which were to be expected during the voyage.

The Gauntlet clipper ship

Editors Note:

The Gauntlet, designed by William Rennie was built in 1853, on the River Clyde. She and the Lord of the Isles also launched that year were considered to be 'the most perfect clipper ships ever launched on the Clyde The Gauntlet "appears more like a yacht of large tonnage than a private merchant ship".[7] Despite being the low cost fare it was also a faster journey than ships direct from Hamburg.[8]

12th October. The food is good and plentiful. We have very good

[7] The Gauntlet Clipper Ship in *London Illustrated News*, Aug 27, 1853, 164
[8] Geitner, Rebekka. *Pers. Com.* 1 October 2014

beef, soup, potatoes, vegetables and white bread - coffee in the morning and tea at evenings. As long as the ship anchors near the shore fresh victuals are delivered aboard every morning. Lest evening we had a quite unexpected, happy moment. Some people standing in a circle not far from us were singing "Sankey" songs in English. Quickly, I took out my "Frohe Botschaft" ("Happy Message") and joined the songs in German. All of us rejoiced in the awareness to be united through the blood of the Lamb. Furthermore, furthermore, a Bible colporteur of the Thames Mission Church came repeatedly aboard and another friendly gentleman visited, accompanied by a German miss who acted as his interpreter. They distributed good reading material especially evangelic magazines. The children received picture cards and very nice little booklets. A reverend of the Church of England arrived and conducted a service after which pamphlets and testaments (English) were given out. Here – as well as on later occasions - we noticed particularly that England contributes in an outstanding way to the spreading of the religious truth. However, many recipients of the valuable books and pamphlets had no other use for them but the most vulgar one. Our hearts were filled with sorrow to see pages of the New Testament scattered everywhere. Some people admitted openly that they had accepted the books not for their contents but for the paper.

At half past five in the evening a tug arrived, the tow rope was belayed and the tug's engine turned over. Smooth and grave our ship glides downstream in the wake of the tug, leaving another foam capped wake behind. Approaching Gravesend, more and more ships of various sizes were sighted and/or passed and the shoreline gradually receded. - Oh, Lord Jesus, master of winds and oceans embrace us with your grace. We beg you to stay at the helm and lead us safely through the perils of the ocean; however - if you decide that the ship will be devoured by the waves - we commit our souls into your hands in the faith that we will land happily here or in eternity.

13th October. We had to anchor again in the sheltered waters abreast of Dale (Editors note: should be Deal)[9] to await the abating of a severe storm at sea in which several ships had perished - as we heard some time later around us I counted 95 ships at anchor. Dale is a very fine city and the glitter of lights along the shoreline is a magnificent sight. It is a wonderful evening and the wonders of Jehovah are unveiled in all their majesty. The nickel of the moon is intermittently covered by racing black clouds - stabbing beams of light from a lighthouse penetrate the darkness in intervals, - stars emerge and disappear again - and the ship is dancing on the crest of the waves. Some people including my dear wife are seasick again. (Prayer follows: "Our Father in heaven ...""")

Sunday 14th October. The weather today is beautiful indeed. The air is quiet, crisp and cold and everything is bathed in the bright sunshine, which really lifts up our spirit. Nearly everybody remained on deck all day until late evening (this is very necessary for the general health). I spent most of the day reading in serenity Gods book. In the afternoon, a dear English brother (co-traveller) by the name of W. Burrel conducted a service on deck and Sankey songs were heard - very popular with the English. His service was moving, presented with much warmth and insight, and had the full attention of the audience. Later on in the evening I met him personally. He is aged, had worked before for some years as a reverend in Australia and is now on the way back to continue his work. He is a member of the Plymouth Brothers who are known as "Bible Christians" and are followers of Darby[10] (Darbyists).

---

[9] Dale is at the approach to Milford Haven waterway, Pembrokeshire whereas Deal is between Gravesend and Dover.
[10] John Nelson Darby (1800-1882) was an influential figure among the original Plymouth Brethren better known as the Exclusive Brethren.

G. Mueller of Bristol is their recent spiritual leader[11] but Darby still has considerable influence by medium of his publications. It is my impression that the English Darbyists are not as limited, exclusive and hard lined as the German ones generally are. This brother was really keen and wrapped up in his vocation to spread the Evangelum amongst the non-believers. We have spent many enjoyable hours together. He told me that he had baptized many converts in the last 12 years. Of course, I had immediately informed him that I am a Baptist.

The Sussex – renamed the Earl in 1913

---

[11] A split between Darby and Mueller in 1848 led to the separation of the Brethren into the exclusive and open branches. This split into two branches was apparently not understood by Pr. Windolf. It explains the different attitudes he witnessed.

16th October. It was stormy and rainy all day yesterday. The weather today was somewhat more friendly in the morning but a strong and cold wind sprang up suddenly at midday. In the afternoon the tug "Sussex-London" towed our ship into open waters. We passed Dover and its chalk cliffs at 5 o'clock. A pity we could not get a glimpse of this romantic town - it was covered in dense fog. However, we could see the lighthouse towering on the highest rook. Many letters were written today to be left with the returning tug.

17th October. During the night, the tug had left unnoticed and our vessel is sailing fast before a favourable wind on a westerly course. Shorelines have disappeared and only the vast circle of the horizon meeting the empty sea is to be seen. The early morning hours are bright but the air is cuttingly cold. Purple seamed morning clouds announce the rising of the sun and soon — the golden globe had emerged from the sea to disperse all remaining dark clouds of the night. In the afternoon the mountain ridges of the Isle of Wight appeared on the horizon - an island famous as the scene of "The Milkmaid" by Richmond. The waters here have already changed to the dark green colour of the deep ocean.

18th October. The hills of Portland - Devonshire - England are gradually emerging on the starboard side. The weather is as fine as usually our days at home are in the month of May, The ships progress is extremely slow - in fact, we are nearly becalmed. In the afternoon it was discovered that a child in the steerage deck was suffering; from Germen measles. Blankets and bedclothes had to be brought on deck to be fumigated with sulphuric ether. The steerage deck had to be evacuated and was fumigated too. All feather beds, quilts or bedcovers filled with downs or feathers were merciless thrown over board accompanied by scream and howls of protest of the owners. We had not taken our feather beds onto the deck but had left then with our other luggage in the cargo hold and were therefore lucky to retain them.

The ship hoisted a yellow flag - the sign that a communicable disease had been discovered aboard - and set course for the coast. In the evening the wind increased and accelerated our speed.

19th October. At daybreak we arrived in the harbour of Plymouth where we had to anchor offshore in a safe distance as prescribed by health regulations. The bight of Plymouth is large and deep and can harbour a vast number of warships. Later, a Dr. Eccles boarded the ship for consultations with our ships doctor. It was decided to have everybody aboard medically examined on the next day. 20th October. All day we had no moment of rest or relaxation. Dr. Eccles boarded the ship in the morning and - assisted by the ship's doctor - medically examined passengers and crew. It was found that two children of different families had contracted the disease and were consequently debarked with all family members to a hospital in the city. All their bedding was burnt. The rumour is now that we have to remain in quarantine for another fortnight and everybody is very depressed.

21st October – Sunday. A stormy, rainy day. The surf beating the rocky foreshore leaves broad, white stripes along the coast. In the afternoon brother BURRELL gave a sermon in English and I conducted a sermon in German in the evening. The majority of Germans aboard were there and listened attentively. Everybody remained on deck throughout the evening and the moon was very bright indeed.

Plymouth Harbour c. 1863

25th October. The past days were very rough - rainy and stormy. At midday - out of the blue - we received the order to pack our goods and chattels for the transport to a hospital ship, as our ship had to be fumigated and cleaned in accordance with health regulations. At 4 o'clock in the afternoon we boarded a small ferry which transferred us to a Navy hospital ship anchored in the far distance. Here we had to remain for the prescribed period of quarantine. We were allowed to move freely and to make use of all sporting facilities of the gymnasium in the upper structure of the ship. The view from here is really splendid. Harbour fortifications are in the foreground - a broad arm of the bight expands to the left and on the right hand side is another broad channel seamed by wooded hills. At the shore and dotted in the hills you can see lovely land houses or villas. Far away at the mouth of the harbour is a lighthouse towering on a rock where the surf continuously breaks into broad stripes of white foam. From the lighthouse a man-made jetty extends further into the sea. In the hills on the right-hand side of the town are more fortifications spreading in an uninterrupted thin line down to the beach. - A lovely panorama indeed!

28th October. Day of the Lord. On the day before yesterday we witnessed a small exercise by the navy, executed with lively gunfire. The services of today were conducted by brother Burrell in the morning, by a missionary from the Plymouth Sailors Mission in the afternoon and by myself in the evening for the Germans. I was furthermore favoured by the Lord to pray and read His Word at the sickbed of a child in the presence of parents, relatives and others.

31st October. The mentioned child has died on Monday morning. The funeral took place at the Plymouth cemetery and I officiated as reverend on request of the ships surgeon since the parents had desired that the funeral service was to be held in the German language. After approximately half an hour in a rowing boat, we arrived at the quay where a hearse was waiting for us. We were driven across the city to the distant cemetery. At the grave, I read a chapter of the scripture and offered a prayer. In the afternoon of the 5th November, we were transported back to the "Gauntlet" after we had passed another medical examination by Dr. Eccles on the 3rd of November. Right after the examination we all had to take a hot bath under supervision. The Plymouth reverend, who had conducted the service eight days ago, again came aboard the "Gauntlet", offered a brief parting sermon and distributed pamphlets in German and English print.

7th November. At midday our ship was towed by a tug into the open sea, we were hardly outside and the waves came up higher and higher and after a few hours we were in the midst of a violent storm. Four days and nights the elements raged with utmost vehemence and the majority of passengers were seasick all the time. On the fourth day all holds of the ship were tightly barred. Wave after wave rolled over the deck with tremendous force - everyone crashing like thunder. Ghastly was the following night when the storm culminated to its peak. Most of us had abandoned all hope of survival; however, the mercy of the Lord was with us. In the early morning hours the towering waves gradually subsided and at daybreak we noticed that we were drifting back towards the English coast. At midday on Sunday the 11th November, we dropped anchor in Portland harbour. The storm had driven us back all the way into the area from where we had started. The ship was badly damaged.

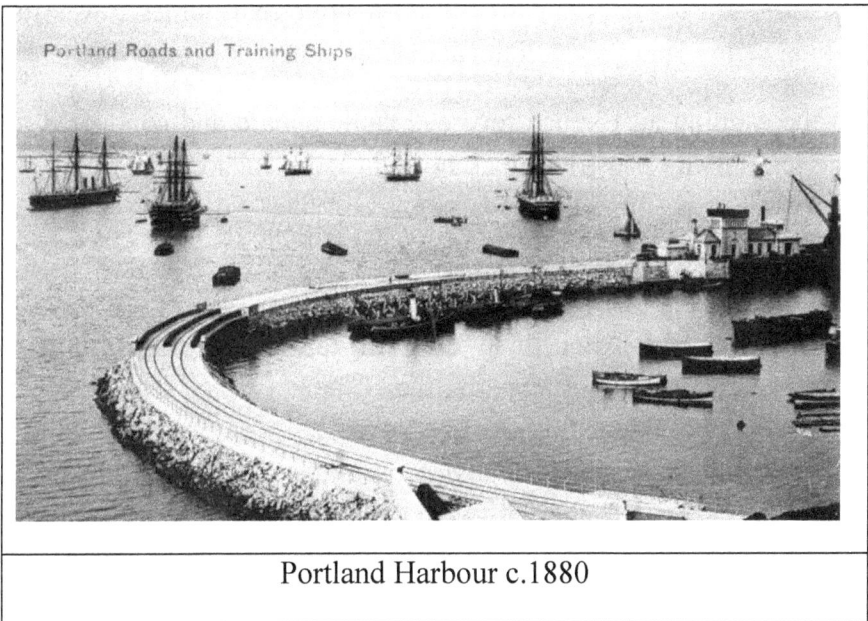

Portland Harbour c.1880

17th November. All hands had been busy during the past days to carry out repairs and restore the seaworthiness of the ship. Here victuals had been taken aboard and we looked forward to the departure with tense expectation. A tug had arrived, the tow rope was belayed and the winch had started to lift the anchor. Suddenly a part of the winch broke and the broken part had to be ferried ashore for repairs - another trial of our patience. We did not regard this as a casual accident but rather looked at the incident as providence of the Lord who had decided for our best. The coast in front of us is of an impressive beauty which is not easy to describe. In closer distance one can see quite clearly single houses, small villages and towns, a railway line... etc. Sometimes a cold mist fills the valleys ashore and drifts only a few feet high above the surrounding waters. Above the distant hills which gently ascend from the shore, the air is clear and green fields and woods are bathed in bright sunshine. On the left the foreshore is steep and rocky - dotted with some fortifications - in the background are villages and towns - and to the right high chalk cliffs tower in white, yellow and grey colours above the water.

In the evening an English reverend came aboard and conducted a service. Finally - at 11 o'clock at night - the anchor was weighed and we were on our way once more.

IV. ON THE OCEAN.

26th. November; After three days of rather uneventful sailing through the calm waters of the Channel, the sea became increasingly rough and on the 21st November we were engulfed by another violent storm. It abated soon and we had two quiet and calm days. The 24th and 25th were extremely rough and the storm reached a vehemence - never experienced before. At 11 o'clock at night, a piercing, thundering crash was followed by hissing and gurgling sounds of masses of water surging into the ship. The first impression was that the ship had struck a cliff or rook and sprung a leak. Expecting the ship to sink within the next moments, I committed my soul into the hands of the Lord; however, He saved us. In the early dawn we saw that the waves had ripped off the main hutch, the whole galley which was situated on deck and one of the lifeboats. All was lost overboard, bilges and cabins where sloshing in feet of water and the waves continued to roll over deck until midday on Sunday. Throughout this time we had to bail water until we were dead tired and too weak to stand on our feet

When the waves finally had subsided, we were full of gratitude and joy and I composed a hymn of thanks which follows underneath:

Tuesday 27th November. Two ships were sighted early in the morning, one - a fourmaster - passed us sailing on opposite course, the other one - sailing in front of us in the same direction - was much slower and soon we overtook and left it far behind.

The days are becoming longer and longer which is a sign that we have reached the more southerly latitudes. For the first time we saw flying fish and at night noticed in particular the wonderful iridescence of the ocean. As far as the eye reaches, the surface glitters with millions of diminutive stars and behind us the wake of the ship is broken into two luminous stripes shining like electric flames.

Far away on the horizon the coast of the island of Madeira passes by and 5 other ships are in sight. The voyage progresses smoothly and the bow of the ship cuts through the waves under full sail - like an arrow.

On the 15th December. We passed the dateline[12] at 9 o'clock in the evening. To mark tho crossing the deck was illuminated and rockets and fireworks were sent up into the sky.

Prevailing Passat winds[13] caused cool and refreshing nights after the heat of the day hours which could be spent under the protection of a tarpaulin rigged over the deck. At night we had always the magnificent sight of the ocean illuminated by millions of lights.

---

[12] (Translators remark: Hr. Windolf obviously refers here to the "dateline" in error - he means the equator. The dateline is the 180th. meridian East/West of Greenwich.

[13] German for trade winds.

Underneath some remarkable experience of the last time:

F. St..., a young miner from the coal pita of Westphalia had been an outstanding personification of evil. This champion of crudeness and blasphemy could not be equalled by others aboard. Initially, it seemed that his animal-like constitution would outlast all mishaps and adversities and nothing whatsoever would touch or move him.

During the storms in the channel, he was suddenly struck down by rheumatic fever. The strong man was as helpless as a new-born babe, could not walk or even stand on his feet and often wept tears in bitter pain. His condition had lasted for several weeks and deteriorated from day to day in spite of all medicines prescribed by the ships surgeon.

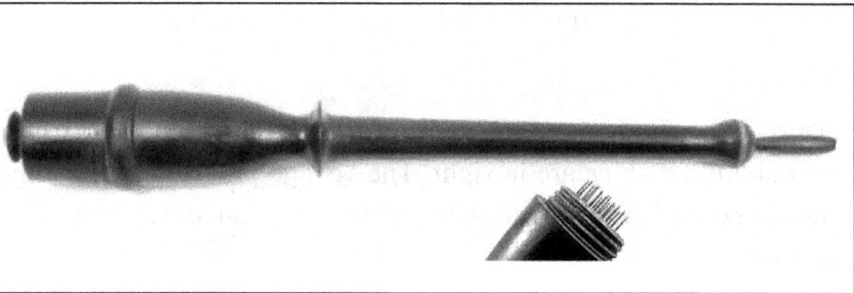

Lebensweker (Life awakener) an instrument invented by Carl Baunscheidt[14]

Suddenly - on one of the past days - he approached us for help, begging humbly for our assistance. I decided to apply the "survivor of life" in form of the "Baunscheidt test" to him. From this hour he

---

[14] The skin was prepared with oils or irritants, the head would be placed over an area of skin. Pulling back and releasing the spring loaded mechanism would puncture the skin with a number of sharp needles. The theory was that this would act as a counter irritant which would distract the body's focus away from the main site of injury, say for example an adjacent abscess. http://phisick.com/item/baunscheidts-lebenswecker-ebony/ Date visited 21 September 2014.

experienced a relief of pain and could move freely for two days. However, soon after he was soaked by rain and contracted a severe cold which aggravated again his suffering. In any case: This godforsaken blasphemer had learned his lesson and had turned to the Lord in his pain. May the Lord save his poor soul!

Another case: Two young German men were involved in a fight during which one of them received a deep and heavy bleeding wound in the head. His opponent was handcuffed and chained in the hold. Here he remained - manacled for four days and nights - and was released only after the ships surgeon had declared that the victim was out of danger and relatives and friends of the culprit had petitioned for his release. May this be a lesson for life for him and may his soul be saved.

27th December. On the day before Christmas the ship was cleaned from top to bottom. All emigrants had to move their belongings up onto the deck at 5 o'clock in the morning and had to remain there until 6 o'clock in the evening. Meals were taken on deck. The day was calm and humid and the following Christmas Day was hot and sultry as well.

The following-days of Christmas day devoted to an uninhibited sequence of days of worldly pleasure. We therefore felt very much out of place, very abandoned and lonesome and longed for the "living in amongst our own people."

12th January. Since my last note, the weather has been continuously rough and cold with intermittent showers and icy winds blowing from the South. For some days the waves have been extremely high.

Many seabirds can be seen, for instance, the albatross (a very large white bird. One was caught, it had a wingspan of 10 feet and the beak measured 8 Zoll[15]), furthermore the cape fowl in black and grey colours and the cape pigeon which is white with bright violet stripes.

Several albatross and cape fowls were caught yesterday (with baited fishhooks). The birds were cruelly tormented by wanton young people before they were finally killed. On the whole, the frivolity and boundless false cheerfulness of many is hard to comprehend. Their crude recitations and theatrical performances are far below all accepted standards of decency and good manners. all this is tolerated and apparently agreed to by the captain and the ship's doctor.

We had favourable weather for some days and made a very fast headway. The average distance for 24 hours was 350 miles - which is an extraordinary fast speed for sailing ships.

On the 25th of January, we passed the ship "Martaban" with emigrants from London for Brisbane aboard at 44^0 - 57' southern latitude and 117^0 - 13' eastern longitude.

4th February; For several days since my last note our speedy progress continued (1155 miles in 3 days)[16] and on the 26th January we passed the cape of Western Australia and on the 29th the most southerly cape of Tasmania, (This is an island which is separated from the southern part of Australia by the narrow and dangerous Bass Strait. We therefore did not go through this strait but circumnavigated Tasmania.

---

[15] Usually 1/12th of a German foot (but could be 1/11th or 1/10th) and the foot varied from 268 to as much as 435mm.

16 "When the Clipper Ship was created, it was the fastest ship ever made. Not only that, but it was huge; it contained more sails than any other and was more than 15 storeys high. Efficient vessels had the ability to cover 2000 miles in a 5 day span, whereas ships before that barely reached 150 miles in a day. This meant that the ships' owners and captains had the ability to earn much more money". http://mcjazz.f2s.com/Clippers.htm. Date accessed 29 September 2014.

Continuous tacking brought us a fair distance further to the north.

Since beginning of February we were becalmed and the ship remained motionless for days. The heat is excessive; everybody feels listless and weak and dreads the possible outbreak of an epidemic fever.

Today, in the afternoon, a small child of an English family has died after weeks of sickness and suffering. The body was given to the sea in the evening in pouring rain.

A short time later, fresh breezes sprang up coming from direction of the land and brought us ahead for minor distances.

During the periods of calm, masses of jelly-fish could be seen drifting through the water near the mirror-like surface.

9th February. Yesterday afternoon we sighted the mountains of New South Wales for the first time – refreshing and encouraging after such a long time of being surrounded by water only. However, the land soon disappeared as the ship had to go on opposite tack. The adverse wind necessitates continuous tacking, progress in very slow and any sailing closer to the coast is too dangerous.

However! ....,.. (A hymn follows).

Every evening is wonderful and the stars of the Southern sky are much brighter than the ones of the Northern hemisphere.

16th February. Now, we have either no wind at all or very light breezes are coming from the opposite direction. The ship is intermittently becalmed or continues on short and slow tacks.

Yesterday was extremely hot again and a thorough cleaning of the ship had been ordered. Women and children had to remain on deck with all our belongings from 5 o'clock in the morning until 6 o'clock in the evening while the men were busy to clean the quarters below. At half past eight in the evening a shark - between eight and ten feet long - was caught and cut into pieces on deck. The power of its tail was quite amazing.

Later on, a threemaster coming from Brisbane passed us a very short distance away. Two more sharks were caught - both larger than the first one.

The wind had increased since sunset but is still unfavourable for our course, nevertheless, we are gradually coming nearer to the coast.

Next morning a dense fog covered the sea. It lifted at 3 o'clock in the afternoon and we had a clear view of the coastline.

Strong winds and rainsqualls prevented the ship from going any closer to the land and we spent the night tacking to and fro on the same course.

At 4 o'clock on Monday morning direct course to the land was set and soon after we sighted Cape Moreton on Moreton Island. A lighthouse on the peak of a mountain showed us the way.

A pilot boarded our ship at 8 o'clock in the morning and was greeted by all with much enthusiasm and tears of joy.

We rounded Moreton Island and arrived in Moreton Buy at midday where the ship dropped anchor. Our "Wonderland" was spread out in front of our eyes: - high and steep mountains, the peaks bare and rocky and bush in the lower regions - some peaks were even covered with clouds.

Almost immediately, fresh fruit and vegetables were delivered: potatoes, carrots, onions, pineapples, bananas, lemons and other rarely known tropical fruit - there seemed to be no end to the pleasant surprises. On Wednesday, the 20th, a tug towed us through the bay and up the Brisbane River into the harbour of Brisbane. All emigrants and their luggage were transferred by ferryboats to a landing near the "emigrant house where we debarked. First, however, we had to bring our luggage into a depot and were than shown to the emigrant house where a meal was served immediately after arrival. All of us were very tired but could hardly sleep owing to the oppressive heat and intermittent thunder-storms lasting throughout the night.

On the 21st. February, Brother Engels from Fassifern Scrub arrived to welcome us in the name of the Community and to lead us to our destination. We left Brisbane in the after-noon by railway for Ipswich where we had to wait for the arrival of our luggage until Saturday afternoon. We found the heat and humidity very oppressing and made here our first acquaintance with the notorious mosquitoes. Brother Engels had wired the time of our arrival from Brisbane, and three brothers with their vehicles were waiting for us at the Ipswich railway station.

Our luggage arrived on Saturday and at midday we started the trip to our new home. After we had travelled for a few miles, a heavy thunderstorm developed and torrential rain soaked us to the skin and made the road impassable. We therefore remained at RESERVE until Monday.

Although I had contracted a heavy cold, I was able to lead the Sunday services - the first time in this new part of the world.

On Monday morning we continued our journey and arrived here (25 English miles from Ipswich) at midday. Many brothers and sisters welcomed us most heartily and we all went to the home of brother and sister RIEK where a table richly loaded with food was uniting to refresh us after the journey. Later on, we were shown to a lovely new house which shortly before had been completed by the community for their future reverend.

More and more brothers and sisters arrived and the evening was devoted to a thanksgiving service and the praise of the Lord. Dear brother HINRICHSEN had composed a song of welcome for the occasion which was beautifully presented by the community.

On reflection - all I can humbly say: "Praised be the Lord......."

Amen, hallelujah

2. THE MINISTRY STARTS

JOURNALISTIC REPORT PUBLISHED IN THE 'WAHRHEITSZEUGE'[17] OF 1879 in a serial Memoir Pages on the Baptist Mission among the Germans in Queensland in Australia [by Hermann Windolf]

Page 98. On Monday the 18th of February 1878, the migrant ship "Gauntlet" under Captain Lucas sailed into Moreton Bay in pouring rain. The same is representative of a large kind of natural safety-harbour and is a refuge for sea travellers around that stretch of the coast. Its lighthouse standing out on the steep mountain crest of forelying Moreton Island, casts the bright rays of its beacons far out into the sea, and is a certain guide for the fisherman passing by on the bleak watery wilderness (showing him) to the shallows of his desired goal. On board the ship, among the hundreds of those on board who were tired of Europe, stood the compiler of this report, not having been driven by greed for gold that perishes, but having become willing to devote his life to the pioneer posts beyond, due to the Macedonian call of some dear brothers in faith in the far south. Under the wise guidance of the pilot, the "Gauntlet" was steered along the right passages to be then anchored quite promptly in a suitable position in the middle of the bay.

There at last lay the land of longing before the enraptured onlookers. Indescribable feelings swell through the human heart at such a moment - any heart which was not deeply moved would be made of stone. Near nineteen long weeks had indeed passed since the departure from West India Docks in London - truly a long spell, during which the eye saw nothing but sky and water. Now all sacrifices and difficulties were forgotten, all the dangers and crises

---

[17] Witmess to the Truth.

of gruesome stormy nights were endured, and the ultimate goal reached. How hardened the heart would be which the sight of the boldly-shaped hills in the distance and the colourful picture of the valleys in the foreground would not bring it into the most joyful mood, and to which this would not appear almost like Paradise after such a long time of deprivation. Houses could also be seen over on the island - single quaint country houses, surrounded by all the charming tokens of the semi-tropical zones flora world. It was not long until a little coaster brought us fresh provisions of nourishment in great abundance: succulent beef, huge potatoes, cabbage, beetroots and carrot etc soup-herbs; furthermore fruit, pears, lovely bananas, delicious ' pineapples, watermelons, and many more - what enjoyment for those familiar with them and what a pleasant surprise for those not acquainted. At the same time the Sanitation Commissioner came on board to examine the condition of the migrant's health. Fortunately, no case of sickness was discovered, which spared us of the boring quarantine period on lonely Peel Island.

The 20th of February was the happy day on which the "Gauntlet" was steered into the mouth of the Brisbane River under the direction of a tugboat, and sailed some 30 English miles all the long way to Brisbane an enchanting journey with its constantly changing scenery on both sides of the river bank. We came up opposite a mission settlement over on the left, where the Gossner mission[18] is making unsuccessful attempts to win the Papua

---

[18] "This was the first mission in what later became Queensland. It was intensively staffed yet surprisingly harmonious, and functioned to facilitate the settlement of Moreton Bay. Some of the Zion Hill missionaries themselves became pioneer farmers of the emerging state of Queensland, imprinting their names on the modern Brisbane map: Rode Road in Chermside and Wavell Heights, Zillman Water Holes, Zillmere, and Zillman Road in Hendra, Gerler Road in Hendra, Franz Road in Clayfield, Wagner Road in Clayfield, Nique Court at Redcliffe, Haussmann Courts and lanes in Meadowbrook (Loganlea) and Caboolture. They are remembered as the first free settlers of Queensland, producing the first free-born settler children in Queensland". It was a combined

negroes[19] for the Gospel. A few of them, about moderate height, stood on the shore and waved to us. These Papuas are on the lowest level of human existence, but they are not only in need of redemption but also able to be redeemed.

Hamilton 1878

At last we sailed up into Brisbane's harbour and anchored. Passengers and their baggage were transported by the steamer to

Lutheran/Presbyterian/Pietist effort with Moravian inspiration and operated between 1838 and 1848. Langbridge, Catherine, Robert Sloan and Regina Ganter. *German Missionaries in Australia* Griffith University http://missionaries.griffith.edu.au/qld-mission/zion-hill-mission-1838-1848. Date accessed 27 September 2014. Zion Hill would have been on the right, not left. What Pr. Windolf is probably referring to is Nerang Creek operated by Pastor Haussmann a former Gossner Missionary. Ganter, Regine. *Pers. Com.* 29 September 2014. At times he was the only advocate for Aboriginal Mission in Queensland. Zion Hill was called German Station at the time Pastor Windolf arrived and later was called Nundah.
[19] The Yaggera aboriginal people.

the landing place at the immigration depot - and we stepped onto the ground of this unknown world.

Brisbane, the capital of Queensland and residence of the Governor, lying at 27 degrees 28'3" latitude and 153 degrees 6'15" longitude, numbers 3500 places of residence and over 30,000 inhabitants. It is a nice friendly city, with thirty places of worship, including four Baptist churches.

It was late summer and the heat due to the long absence of rain was very burdensome for us. All the first night, which we spent with all the others in the immigration building, a fearful storm broke out. They are far heavier here than in Germany and have a beneficial influence on the climate and state of health of the people. In the morning of the next day, a friendly "angel" appeared to us in the form of brother Eder sent from the fifty-six miles removed German brethren, to greet us and lead us to our destination. By means of the railway, we rode the fifty six English miles to Ipswich - a healthy, rapidly growing country town with 5200 inhabitants, among them a good number of German ones. The town is provided with gas and water by pipe, has a Grammar school, seven churches, among them a German one, several businesses, hotels, hospitals, an important wool factory (spinning and weaving) two newspapers. In the local district (West Moreton) the German element is numerously represented. Fassifern Scrub, my destination, being one of the best farming areas of the colony, spreading out over many miles and also bordering on a good parish, numbers for example 150 German farmers together with the occasional English one, and they are turning thick scrub into the richest estates with much effort but singular success. No Englishmen dares to undertake such a huge task - to transform the scrub with its soil type well suited for agriculture, into good property. This was left for the German with his persistent diligence to reach achievements of recognition in this sphere of work. A great deal of energy and will is needed to set down in the middle of the scrub, often without amenities, but where one can acquire property from the Government under very favourable conditions, for one's own.

Editors Note: Aub Podlich a Lutheran pastor whose "people were scrub Germans" with roots in the Kalbar area citing long standing local sayings[20] wrote of Fassifern Scrub, "The Lutheran churches of the Kalbar-Boonah area began when the state government threw open the 'useless' scrublands on the old pastoral runs for closer settlement in 1877 and propagandised thousands of 'German fools' to take up selections that others had rejected as too difficult. The Germans, mainly from West Prussia, Pomerania and Brandenburg, were lured by the prospect of owning their own 80-acre blocks, and they streamed out of the port of Hamburg across the seas to Queensland in their thousands. They were people whose prospects in their homelands were so bleak they were prepared to risk everything in incredibly difficult conditions where there were not yet towns or amenities and only the tracks of the Yugarapul people through their ancestral scrub homelands. Many of their descendants are still here. In the space of ten years of hacking, crashing and burning, the Germans cleared the scrubs and converted the area into a patchwork of scrub-soil farms, highly prized today.[21]

Murray Johnson and Kay Saunders in their history of the Boonah region state, **"**Government legislation which fragmented the large pastoral runs paved the way for closer settlement of the Fassifern Valley. The fact that much of the area excised from Dugandan and Fassifern runs was without surface water and consisted of virgin scrub also made it very affordable for settlers hungry to have land of their own. Among other things, the Crown Lands Act of 1868

---

[20] Podlich, Aub. *Pers. Com*. 23 September 2014.
[21]Podlich, Aub. Obum Scrub in *The Lutheran*, May 2005.

was the first legislation to specifically use the terms 'selector' and 'selection', words which have reverberated to the present day and can rightly be applied to those who settled in the northern Fassifern Valley. Sub-divided into landholdings up to 160 acres in extent, prices ranged from two shillings sixpence to a maximum of three shillings nine pence per acre. By meeting five annual instalments and effecting improvements consisting of a basic dwelling, fencing and the cultivation of 10 percent of the area, selectors gained freehold tenure."[22]

---

[22] Johnson, Murray and Kay Saunders. *Working The Land, An Historical Overview of Boonah and its Northern District* (Sunnybank Hills: State of Queensland, 2007)

Clearing the Fassifern Scrub

The laws of domicile settlement allow every adolescent worker to take up 80 to 160 acres of good land. As soon as such a one has made his selection from the open land and the same is accepted in the Lands Office, he has to pay the initial annual rate of 6 pence (50 schilling) per acre and four further annual payments complete the sale price (2 ½ shillings equals DM2.50 per acre). But there is a condition that the selector himself lives and works on the land during these five years, and builds a dwelling place and barn and makes a tenth of the land arable. A similar law determine the condition by which one can acquire land otherwise (without having to reside on it himself), in far larger stretches (are available) through ten year term rate payments of 5 to 15 pence per acre. The most important German settlement is Rosewood Scrub[23] (12 miles from Ipswich), over 100 English square miles in extent and in which a few thousand Germans are said to live, alongside a small number of English. The size of a farm varies from 40 acres up to 400 acres or more.

German farming family in Fassifern Valley c.1890

---

[23] Now Marburg.

After a two day stay in Ipswich, we set out for Fassifern Scrub. Some brothers had arrived from there with their own vehicles in order to convey us and our baggage along the thirty mile stretch back there. The weather was unbearably sultry, like the day before. Hardly had we set out and driven a few miles, when a mighty storm broke out. The pouring rain necessitated us to seek shelter in a lone house by the wayside — it was the home of brethren Z. who were farming land by lease. For the first time we stepped into an Australian farming homestead, built of timber throughout. As soon as the rain let off a little, we rode on further. The bend to the left led us into the wides, which in contrast to the scrub describes above, is sparser occupied with mainly large trees. What struck us was the number of dry woodland trees extending their bare tops lamenting towards the sky - a result of the year-long drought. In places, dry grass was covering the sparse earth, while in between, large vaulted oven shaped anthills met the eye, and I first took them for blocks of stone, which they are not unlike. When hollowed out, they serve as baking ovens for the farmers, who bake the most tasty wheat- bread in them. Meanwhile, we saw the Australian "springing mouse" - kangaroo (4 to 5 feet high) making his leaps. Once again I saw them in big packs - armies of them. Since the Government has been paying a high premium for each scalp, they have become rare in districts that are settled. A successful hunter earns 15 to 20 shillings (1 shilling equals IDM) a night, not infrequently. The persistent rain hindered our progress a lot, especially as the horses had gone right downhill due to the drought. Although another brother and myself walked the whole way by foot, the vehicle was only able to proceed slowly, so that we deemed it necessary to make a halt at nightfall on Ipswich Reserve, halfway towards our goal. Brethren K live here, and we soon felt better under their hospitable roof. As the coming day was a Sunday, we spent our first Sabbath here in the circle of the few brethren who had gathered together for worship — something we had not quite planned on. This place, where a goodly number of (our) members had resided, had once seen some good times as here the first conversion had taken place. One after the other they had gradually shifted to new settlements (Fassifern, Mt Walker, Rosewood etc) right down to two families. The ministering of God's Word on my part was done under extreme bodily weakness. The change of climate, the unaccustomed heat, moreover a total saturation from walking in a wet suit, had led to as extremely painful and weakening attack of dysentery, which was to hold me in the most painful arena of suffering for weeks to come.

Continued on Page 106 (next month's issue). On Monday the 25th February the sun was shining brightly, quickly scattering the thick cloud cover. We rode on Brother L's highly spirited horses once again towards our future place of living. On the way, we came across a large grassy plain spreading out for miles and through which a creek flowed. Here the eye enjoys a rewarding farness of sight. To the right in the foreground, the friendly good looking guesthouses and residential buildings of Normanby Station stand out. One can gain a rough estimate of the extent and value of such a cattle station when one learns that in this colony of Queensland alone, there are more than 1600 stations of various sizes many of which are 100 and a few 200 square miles (Eng) in size, and serve as grazing grounds for herds of cattle and even more sheep, in their thousands; in the background, the sugarloaf shaped rock- crowned crest of Mount Walker boldly and freely [towers?] over the hill country bordering the station. At the left, one sees Harrisville in the foreground and Pic Mountain[24] in bold outlines behind it. Just to the back of this, one's view is arrested surprisingly by the grotesque contours of a high mountain chain, the Main Range. In front of this are the wooded heights of a broad

---

[24] Possibly the Peak Crossing area. Douglas, Karen Fassifern District Historical Society *Pers. Com.* Sept 30, 2014.

valley-basin. Just below these sharply marked mountains lies Fassifern Scrub. When the grass plain was passed aver, the way led through the woods again, past isolated farm homesteads. One big fish pound was totally dried out and many skeletons of cattle and horses were strewn there. During extended drought, cattle dragged themselves to such watering places, and often remained stuck and came to an end in their slimy hollows. Here I saw for the first time those remarkable plants peculiar to Australia called Grasstrees. A bush of reed like grass of unusual strength and size sprouts out at suitable areas from the ground, forming a treelike shaft consisting of a resinous bituminous substance, growing (under favourable conditions) out to 10 to 12 feet in diameter and up to 8 to 12 feet high, or higher, wearing a thick crown of luxuriantly developed band—like grass (6 to 7 feet long), in whose centre a blossom stem shoots up perpendicularly for 8 to 10 feet.

It is interesting that it appears here, as one would conclude that they would occur more abundantly in the vicinity of well watered ground on levels. However on we went over grass-covered hill country in which a farmhouse was visible here and there. A few miles further still, and we were riding along a river like expanse of water called a lagoon. These often stretch out for many miles in sunken pools, then suddenly stop. The one lying before us, called Kent's Lagoon, or Devil's lake by the blacks, is said to be six or seven miles long and abounds in fish (eels). Now Fassifern Scrub also lay before us; a bend to the right led us into it, and for the first time in our life we trod through this mysterious virginal forest thickness of trees known by the term of 'scrub'. In the hard working hands of diligent farmers the romance of this original forest began to fade, and will vanish in several years. Huge hundred foot high forest giants of the hardest type of timber are surrounded by under growth of various heights. Occasionally, the bottle tree can be found, so called because of its bottlelike shape, whose bulk is similar to the German oak and whose timber is soft like a sponge, and last year served as nourishment for the cattle. Vines wind upwards to the branches of the highest trees from which they often hang down to the earth in a thin twine of sixty feet long or more. There is however, also a kind which has the thickness of a man's body, unusually twisted and knotted. It is noteworthy that the timber types of the scrub are sharply distinguished from those of the forest so that a transition from one to the other is apparent as a sharp dividing line related to the consistency of the soil. We had to ride about three miles through this forest, which was to become our home territory. The vehicle pulled up at a clearing to the left of the track - it was the settlement of brother R. The homestead was soon reached by a ride through some corn plantations, friendly faces greeted us on the way, and we then proceeded into the house, to the table liberally spread with drinks and food. The devout conversations of friendly brothers added taste to the banquet. Then we went in triumph to the newly built pastor's manse nearby.

Representation of the first Kalbar chapel

Not far from there stands the chapel. Both are simple unadorned and built of wood, to their type in this country. The floor was raised on stumps which are fixed in the ground and which support the doorsteps as well. They come up one to two feet above the ground. Roughly carpentered floor boards support the uprights. The walls are either overlain with sawn planks (for the house) or covered with roughly carpentered thick planks (for the chapel), the roof being covered with timber shingles. Somewhat removed is the fireplace (kitchen), likewise built of timber. The house and chapel stand on a so called pocket (i.e. a natural grasspatch in the middle of the bush), overshadowed by a grove of cedar trees.

German Baptist Ministers

With thanks to the Lord, we entered this house, meant for us, and made the first necessary installations. In the evening, a preliminary welcome was put on by the brethren, who gave a thanksgiving meeting in the chapel. Brother H (Henrichsen) had composed a long anthem for this, which was then sung. Wednesday evening found us gathering again with the brethren for the prayer meeting in the chapel. On Saturday, 2nd March, in an unusually full members meeting, brother Krueger and Peters relinquished their tasks as leaders of the congregation of Fassifern and Mount Walker respectively, showing me that I had been unanimously elected in a previous business meeting as teacher and elder of both congregations and that the brethren had obliged themselves to take care of my upkeep. After I had expressed the feelings of my heart in prayer, and accepted this choice before the Lord, the further direction of the proceedings was laid on me. They had saved the examining and admitting of six new young converts for my arrival. Their testimonies to the grace of God experienced in their hearts were so definite, that we were able to gladly comply with their wish and accept them as candidates for baptism. Midnight was long gone by the time we had finished this sacred task, and each went with hope to his own home.

On the 8th March, I took the opportunity of riding in a two wheeled cart belonging to Brother D. to Mt Walker (16 miles). This kind of vehicle which is best for making progress in this territory was unusual to me and made me quite weary. On the following day, a storm brought the desired rain, which kept up all that night and the whole Sunday and hindered us from going to the chapel. Around midday Brother R arrived from Fassifern by horse, bringing the sorrowful news of the unexpected and sudden departure of Sister Peters. She had just recovered from having a baby boy the week before, and just a few days afterwards, the child had died, and now she herself was suddenly called away. This painful message obliged me to hurry away without hesitation, as the next day was to be her funeral. One of the brothers lent me a horse, and we then began the journey back in the heavy rain, taking the shortest way through the bush. Unused to riding, the journey over the slippery terrain became quite unpleasant, but the dear Lord helped us to reach Fassifern without incident, even though fully soaked.

The next day, at noon, the brethren came together from near and far, relatives and neighbour in great numbers, gathering in the house of the bereaved. The grieving husband was very downcast. Introduced the funeral service in this home with some singing, read 2 Corinthians 5:1-9, and prayed. After another hymn, I took up the text of Revelations 14:13, directing another word of comfort from Matthew 18:12 to those who were weeping, to close. After another prayer, and hymn number 614, the procession set in motion to the open grave in the garden where there was some singing and praying once again. As the grave was being filled in, we sang the victory hymn of the resurrection (430) a brother prayed once again, and we parted with hymn 296. Days and weeks of serious suffering, the result of my repeated saturation now commenced. However, the Lord blessed the cures which were applied and granted a gradual recovery. My illness was a strength-sapping state of fever, coupled with dysentery. Only with the greatest effort could I lead a members meeting, give a wedding speech, and take several other meetings as well in this time. Thanks be to the Lord for his gracious enabling.

On 7 April, being in the way to recovery, I could again hold the Sunday services, in which the Lord blesses us. On the 4th, Brother H. Schneider had been called home, (used to live 21 miles away) having been the most important proponent of our work since its beginning in 1862. According to the testimonies of the brothers, he had been a man of warm devotion of heart. Unfortunately his views did not totally agree with ours, as in Germany he had belonged to and served in the Schauffler fellowship.[25] Much unrest had arisen because of this. However, the good and beautiful outweighs the imperfect. May his remembrance be blessed. Up to 12 April, I made some home visits, lead a business session and other church services. On the 13th April I rode by horse to Mt Walker, still very unaccustomed to this way of travelling. Several brothers accompanied me. In the evening I led a very important business meeting there, and also the afternoon meeting on the following Lord's Day, speaking on Hebrews 13: 7 and 8, with regard to Brother Schneider's home coming. Four mothers had also turned up in the chapel to have their children blessed, a practice which had taken place earlier here, the procedure being that the layman had taken the child in his arms, cuddled and kissed it, asking for the name of the child at the same time, and blessed it by laying his hands on it. We have no comment from the Lord for such ceremonies, and it is a false custom little better than infant sprinkling. Naturally I could not stand for this, so I had number 140:1, 2 sung, read Matthew 19: 13-15 proving that the Lord alone blesses the child, and that we should not seek to rob him of His glory and omnipotence, that we could lay the child in our arms in faith in his Word, in united prayer and thus be sure of his blessing on the child. After that I visited two sick-beds, read and prayed with the sick brothers and give a lesson on Psalm 91 for our edification.

---

[25] Presumably associated with William G Schauffler who came from a German colony near Odessa, went to Andover Seminary in the USA, then spent most of his life in Constantinople. "He was not very successful as a missionary as for as conversions are concerned, but he did monumental work in linguistics and translation." .Maxfield, Charles A. *Pers Com.* Oct. 22, 2014. His strong views on Sabbath observance may have been the issue that caused trouble. Schauffler, William G. *Autobiobraphy of William G Schauffler* (New York. Anson D.F, Randolf and Company: 1887) 55-57. More likely is a heritage of German Pietism where lay people regularly met in small groups to pray and encourage each other. Maxfield, Charles A. *The Creation of the United Church of Christ in South Dakota.* Dec. 1989. http://www.maxfieldbooks.com/ UCCinND.html#S2d. Date accessed Oct 27, 2014.

3. THE LIFE, WRITINGS AND WORK OF HERMANN WINDOLF 1846-1922

By Glenn Roberts, June 1986.

On the 19th May, 1846 in the town of Grunenplan, Germany, an eleven day old child, called Friedrich Wilhelm Hermann was christened in the local Lutheran church. It seems he was the first child of the family, his father being Friedrich Wilhelm Conrad, a master mason, and his mother Marie-Wilhelmine Agnes, who bore him at 23 years of age. Four sisters and two brothers were to follow. Sometime between the birth of the first sister, Anna Mathilda Marie in 1848 and the second, their father swung over to the new evangelical movement known as Baptists. (These details were all copied from the above church register in March 1984 by some unknown person and entered in the Baptist archives in Hamburg, to be discovered later that year.) But what makes this so remarkable? This lad, known by his name Hermann, was to be baptised by immersion at 16 years of age, by a Baptist pastor Kipperberg, enter a mission school in Hamburg three years later, probably under the encouragement of his uncle Heinrich - a harbour missionary, and after being trained under the leader of the movement, J.C. Oncken, ministered in his own country for over a decade before migrating to a remote missionfield called Australia.

The location of Hermann's first pastorate in Germany at age 22 was Herford, in Westphalia. This was from 1868 to 1870. He held daily revival prayer meetings and baptised converts as young as 10 and 13 years old.[26] An historian of this church, W. Riemenschneider, described his as "of a quite meek disposition, extending love to the poor and needy" and conducting baptisms at different stations, especially of young people.[27] Hermann's pen had also become quite active in ministry, as can be seen from the

---

[26] *Missionblatt* 1868, 106. 1869, 32.
[27] *Solchen Schatz* 1965, 31.

titles of three sermon collections he published in these years, as well as a poem on the events of the time in Biblical perspective, which he dedicated to the Kaiseress Augusta.[28]

A motion moved by Oncken at the Northwest Union conference promoted Hermann to the Braunschweig (Brunswick) area where he served for another 9 years or so, marrying in the meantime. An enquiry to the present day Baptist church in that city, where records have survived, shows that no mention is made of him, but his work there is confirmed by Windolf in his journals.

Due to pressures and war in the country, many were migrating to freer lands under assisted passage and otherwise, and the young pastor felt a call to follow some of them to Australia in late 1877. He and his wife, both aged 31, and two children Frederich (3) and Hannah (1) sailed from Hamburg via London and reached Moreton Bay in 19 stormy weeks, during which he kept a vivid diary which is preserved in "Der Pilger" (*The Pilgrim*). 1879 p. 6ff

They were classed as "free settlers".[29] Their arrival on 20th February, 1878 was celebrated with joy by the Baptist settlers and Windolf, being a true journalist, is best left to describe it for himself:

"It was late summer, and the heat due to long absence rain was very burdensome to us; on the first night, which we spent with all the others in the immigration quarters, a fearful storm broke. These are heavier than those in Germany and have a beneficial influence on the climate and the people's state of health. On the morning of the next day, a friendly angel in the form of br. E(der) appeared to us, sent from the 56 mile distant German brethren at Fassifern Scrub.. "

---

[28] *Australian Baptist* Nov 1930, 9.
[29] Queensland State Archives, Passenger Lists for the "Gauntlet".

The description of his journey through Ipswich and Normanby Reserve contain incredible detail. He reports that later "bros. Kruger and Peters laid down their positions as leaders of the assemblies of Fassifern Scrub and Mt. Walker respectively, showing me that I had been elected as teacher and elder of both". All began well, but by August that year Windolf had disagreed severely with the same lay-leaders over handling of monies for a new worker to be sent over from the homeland. The reasons he gives to the "Pilger" magazine are different: "the admittance of members was often made too lightly - there was a lack of sound and thorough grounding - now they group themselves together under the leadership of a man capable of unbridled ego and greed for power, claiming to be a church"!

German Settlers, Rosewood Scrub c. 1880

Consequently, the 1st of January 1879 saw Windolf installed in the "geographical centre" of the mission field - Rosewood Scrub (now Marburg). Though the group there then numbered 96, by 1st January 1880, 47 had been excluded and nine lost through other reasons leaving only 58! This indicates a severity of discipline on Windolf's part. His fervent activity is shown by this report to Br. Brucker of the "Pilger": "In the 1st quarter of 1879 I preached the saving Word of God in 60 meetings, led 31 prayer meetings, gave a funeral message, served 4 times at the breaking of bread, and made 70 home visits", most of which were done on horseback! Obviously he was trying to take on too much.[30] The actual minutes at Marburg only begin on 16th May 1880 (Pentecost) when the Bethel chapel opened there. They are recorded in Windolf's handwriting up to March 1883, revealing much of his thinking and attitudes; for example, an admonition against unduly long prayers.

In spite of the break that had been made with Fassifern Scrub (Engelsburg), real times of revival were experienced at Marburg. For instance, in Easter of 1881 at Tarampa Scrub's "Zoar" chapel, where a revival meeting after a Lovemeal continued till daybreak, 19 souls were won over to the Gospel, followed by 32 next Sunday after a public baptism. [31] However, strain and poor health got the better of him. In July of 1882, Windolf negotiated peace and reconciliation with Fassifern where he had served previously on the agreement that old issued be not entered into. His last entry in the Marburg minutes describes his concern for the continuation of the work there:'

"He would in no way let God's work suffer in favour of temporal things - on the contrary! It was painful for him.... due to his suffering, to give his position up... agreed that we should have another worker to help in the great field of labour for both churches (including Brisbane River), br. Windolf would take it on

---

[30] *Der Pilger* 1879, 94. He gave his address as P.O. Frederichs, via Rosewood.
[31] *Wehrheitszeuge* Sept 5, 1881,

himself to (write to) Germany in this regard." (He often wrote of himself in the third person).

From this point, Windolf's pastoral ministry recedes for a while, and his writing ministry comes to the fore. The first issue of the Pilger for 1884 carries a poem by him called "Under the Cross", and a few months later, a commemorative poem of his was chosen to appear with the obituary of J.G. Oncken in this magazine, showing that his standing as a Christian poet was already acknowledged in the German speaking world. It was three years later though that his first printed anthology appeared on the market:- "Thautropfen" (Dewdrops) from a publisher in Bonn, of which two samples are preserved in the Pilger.

However, except for a few references in the minutes of the German conference churches, Windolf's name and pen is silent for over a decade. We can deduce however, that he pursued a quite "behind - the - scenes ministry in these years, being instrumental in calling further pastors over e.g. M. Bernoth[32] (1885) and S. Bluhm in 1900. In 1901, a literary surprise appeared: a collection on Oncken's sermons from notes that Hermann (and his uncle

Pr. Michael Bernoth 1868

---

[32] Pastor Bernoth withdrew from the German Baptists and was rebaptised as a 7th Day Adventist c. 1893. http://sqheritage.adventist.org.au/history date accessed 29 September 2014.

Heinrich) had taken down decades before and brought over with him, entitled "Licht und Recht" (Light and Justice), was sent back to be published by the Baptist publishing house at Kassel, and is prefaced by him. Also, a similar work by the Jewish convert [Julius] Kobner[33] was put out by Windolf. [34]

New German Baptist Church. Marburg with tent for Conference meals. 14' Sept 1905

But a revival in ministry was soon to come. A paper in the 1904 conference booklet records Windolf's fervour on keeping the "Sabbath" showing he was alive and well, and in 1905, he was "festively reinstalled" as pastor in Marburg. He revised list of

[33] J.G. Oncken, J. Kobner and G.W. Lehmann formed the triumvirate, the "Kleeblatt" whose devoted work led to founding of Baptist churches throughout Germany" Payne, Ernest A. Julius Kobner and the German Baptists in *The Baptist Quarterly* 389. UD. http://www.biblicalstudies.org.uk/pdf/bq/04-8_380.pdf. Date accessed 29 September 2014.
[34] *Queensland News Budget*. Deutsche Beilage, Sept 8, 1911.

members their numbers 81. During this second pastorate he continued as reporter for the conference to the "Wahrheitszeuge" over the next two years, By 1908 he had a new lease of life: another anthology appeared called "Psalmenklange" (Sounds of Psalms)[35] and he commenced a series of ministry trips to the Kingaroy area which are described in "Deusche Beilage" - German supplement to the Queensland News Budget of Aug. 29th, 1908. Thirty years of his ministry in Queensland was celebrated the same year[36] when he was sixty-two years of age.

At some stage Windolf must have also studied up homeopathic medicine, which become evident from notices in the "Deutsche Beilage" where his cure for diphtheria is mentioned. Mechanics and architecture were also part of his repertoire, according to his grandson Henry, who claims that books on these subjects were left from his grandfather's library, and even contained some of his own design!

In 1909, Windolf resigned from Marburg, being replaced by pastor Ehmke, and went to live with his son near Engelsburg. There he continued his writings and the next year saw the publication of two further anthologies: Sonnenstrahlen" (Sunrays)[37] and "Efeu und Himmelsschussel" (Ivy and Primroses). Copies of both of these have survived. In 1911, another one - "Unter Maien und Palmen" (Among Mayflower and Palm Trees) appeared, but it is now not extant. The Queensland News Budget, now held in the Oxley Library, gives us such fine details as a stroke in December-1911 and a fall from a vehicle in July 1912 which Windolf suffered in his old age. Undeterred though, he put out two more collections of poems in 1913: "Aus Hohen und Tiefen" (From heights and depths) and "Heimatwarts" (Homewards), the latter

---

[35] A copy is held in the Australian Lutheran College. Lohe Memorial Library.
[36] *Wahrheitszeuge* 1908, 183.
[37] A copy of this book is held in the State Library of Queensland.

indicating his looking forward to the heavenly home. Both of these were acclaimed by the Governor of Queensland and the chancellor of the University. He was well known by this time in Germany as a poet. This genius even delved into horticulture and became an honorary member of the "Luther Burbank Society" of California, distributing their pamphlets in Queensland.[38] As well, a new anthology called "Glockentone" was produced, despite the war, and copies were shipped to this state.

Herman Windolf in old age

---

[38] *Queensland News Budget* July 18, 1914.

By 1921 Windolf had put out a selection of hymns and poems for "recitation at all kinds of festive occasions". But this was to be his last work, for by 22nd February, the next year his pen was stopped forever, following a stroke. He was survived by a wife, and three generations, but also by many literary jewels, many of which remain untranslated. He was buried in a humble grave at the Kalbar public cemetery.

4. RECOGNITION OF PR. WINDOLF AS A HYMN WRITER

From Burrage, Henry S. *Baptist Hymn Writers And Their Hymns*. Portland: Brown Thurston & Company, 1888, Page 532-534

HERMANN WINDOLF. 1846 -.

Hermann Windolf was born at Grunenplan, Duchy of Brunswick, Germany, April 28, 1846. He was converted when sixteen years of age, and united with the Baptist church at Einbeck, in Hanover. Through the mission paper published at Hamburg, and Der Sendbote, he became interested in missions, and love for his Master awakened in him a desire to be employed in the work of giving the gospel to the heathen. But it pleased the Lord, he says, to keep him in the school of patience, and teach him lessons which would be useful to him in the work upon which he was to enter. His father was a mason, and he served an apprenticeship with him. He received instruction also in an institute of technology. In 1865, he attended the theological school at Hamburg, with which at that time Oncken and Klibner were connected. He studied the Gospel of John under Oncken. Not less stimulating and faithful, he says, was the instruction of Klibner. Returning to his trade, he devoted a part of his time to evangelistic work. For two years (1867- 1869) he labored as a missionary at Herford, in Westphalia. From 1873, to 1877, he performed a like service in Brunswick. At the close of 1877, he sailed with his family for Queensland, Australia, where he landed February 20, 1878.

During the remainder of that year he served the German Baptist church at Fassifern and Mount Walker as pastor. From 1879, to 1884, he was pastor of the German Baptist church at Marburg and Upper Brisbane River. On account of impaired health he was laid aside for a year and a half. Since 1886, he has been pastor of the German Baptist church at Engelsburg. His ministry has been greatly blessed in the conversion of souls, and four new chapels have been erected in connection with his labors.

His first hymn was written when he was eighteen years of age, during a period of sickness. In all, he has written about two hundred hymns, many of which have appeared in different Baptist papers, and some of them in collections of hymns, for example, "Die Glaubensharfe " and " Die Zionsklange." In 1886, a collection of his poems and hymns, entitled "Thautropfen auf dem Pilgerwege" was published in Bonn on the Rhine. The volume received the favorable notice of Karl Gerok and several other well known German poets. Gerok says, "It well deserves the name 'Thautropfen', since the face of Jesus Christ is mirrored therein in manifold colors, like the sun in the pearls of the morning." Mr. Windlolf is represented in the "Glaubensharfe" by three hymns. One of these is a translation of Lyte's Abide with me! Fast falls the eventide. (Translated hymn follows)

In "Die Zionsklange " Mr. Windolf has fourteen hymns, although four are not credited to him.

The hymnal of the New Apostolic Church includes one hymn (No. 386) by Herman Windolf (the Apostolic Cathedral at Hatton Vale is part of this group). The tune it is sung was written by Winton James Baltzell and is found in *Songs of Grace and Glory* Volume 2 , No. 187.

O Love, The Golden Sunshine Bright

O love, the golden sunshine bright,
of weary human hearts,
when in my soul it sheds its light
all pain from me departs.
The darkness fades and night must flee
where Jesus' love doth shine
and peace and happiness flow free
within the hearts that pine.

Refrain

O love of God, so full and true,
of ancient time, yet ever new.
It lives for me, it lives for you
and draws us all to Him anew.

2
When from the cross that ray of love
pierced through my night of sin
and brought me sunshine from above,
I woke to God within.
Since then I know who loved me true,
yes, even unto death.
My heart shall now His will pursue,
praise Him in ev'ry breath!

Refrain

3
The Sun that shines my fears to quell
and offers bliss to me
is Jesus, my Immanuel,
for all eternity!
I'll sing to Him my joyful song
while in this vale of tears
and ever with the heav'nly throng
when He to me appears.

5. THE BEGINNINGS OF THE GERMAN BAPTIST WITNESS
By Rev. John White, M.A.

The colony of Queensland was destined to be considerably influenced by Christian German migrants and their families. Indeed, the influence had started to operate before the colony was separated from New South Wales in 1859.

The formal establishment of Baptist work in Queensland was due to the Baptists who came to the colony in 1849 under the British migration scheme which had been promoted by Rev. Dr. John Dunmore Lang. However, that work was indebted to the prior activity of the earliest German settlers, and was to be further indebted to the direct contribution made by many of these after the first church was formed in 1855.

It is one of the mysteries of providence why people should elect to leave their homeland to settle in a new and untamed land. If we believe in an active divine purpose in all things, we can thank God for his leading, by which so many Christians were moved to come to this colony.

As for the German migrants in the mid-1900s and later, there were some understandable reasons. In short. life in Europe had serious economic, social and religious disadvantages. The coming of industry and the decline of agriculture had an unsettling effect. Life became more difficult for a people of the land. The social changes were irksome. Military demands were growing for a people who loved their land and were content with their work in peaceful and quiet conditions. Religious persecution was not unknown.

Under the circumstances, the burgeoning forth of life in the new world would be pictured as a dream come true. Reports circulating told of its climate and soil, its facilities and freedom, and its gold. Immigration officers sold this vision, and by the mid-1800's were attracting large numbers, including some thousands who then or later came to Queensland. They were to find the great benefits, but also the hardships of pioneering life.

The first Germans to come to Queensland were a truly apostolic twelve, together with their families. They also came as a result of the work of Dr. Lang. He had gone overseas to enlist missionaries for the proposed evangelising of the aborigines of the Moreton Bay area. Failing to find them in Britain, he turned to a group trained in Germany for missionary purposes in the school of the Lutheran, Dr Johannes E. Gossner, who had founded a missionary society in 1836.

These missionaries became the first free white settlers in the Moreton Bay area. In 1824 a penal settlement had been set up. It closed in the early 1840s. The first of the missionaries landed at Humpy Bong, near the present Redcliffe, in March 1838. Later, they transferred to the Nundah area. There, on Zion's Hill, and adjacent to Kedron Brook, they built rough houses, a school and a chapel. The mission work was full of difficulty and was closed by 1850. The period, it is noted, bridged the days of penal and free settlement.

It is interesting to observe that when the Mission closed, only five of the original missionaries were still associated with it. Three of these, together with one who had come to reinforce the mission strength, can be certified as having Baptist leanings, and later, definite Baptist affiliations. They were Zillman, Franz, Rode and Gerler. They had links with the Wharf Street Baptist Church, formed in 1855, and the work at Hendra (now Clayfleld) which started in 1869.

These Christian leaders may well have served to influence migrants to come to Queensland. After the Mission closed, they found settlement on the land or in trade, and were deeply attached to the land of opportunity. The reports of their experiences, if not their personal appeal, would dispose many to join them. In the event, from whatever motive, Germans who were, or were to become, Baptists arrived in large numbers from the 1850's and into the 1870's.

Following the initial settlement in the vicinity of German Station (Nundah), these migrants were scattered in several directions. Some stayed around Brisbane. Some moved south towards Logan to engage in farming pursuits. Some probably moved towards Caboolture. The greater number, however, moved towards Ipswich. Some halted at Redbank Plains. Most, however, had the intention of seeking the rich lands of the Brisbane and Bremer Rivers. They were ultimately to find their homes in a wide surrounding circle, and to form many thriving churches.

An interesting development, relating to the whole German work from the early days, was based on a link sustained with the Ipswich church. A special and much appreciated interest was shown by the Rev. T.S. Gerrard, the Ipswich pastor during the years 1869-1874. He probably welcomed them as they passed through the town. .In 1869, one of the groups sought fellowship with the Ipswich church and asked for whatever ministry it could offer. This was repeated by the group from Normanby in the following year.

This enquiry was the small beginning of fellowship which led to the formation of the first Association of Baptist Churches in Queensland. It linked the Ipswich church with the fellowships of Brisbane River, Normanby Reserve, Mt Walker, Rosewood Scrub and Fassifern Scrub. .

At some time before 1875, conferences were initiated by 'The South Queensland German Baptist Union.' This was later to become 'The Conference of German Baptist Churches in Queensland.' It was the formation of this Association between Ipswich and the churches of the surrounding area which stirred action leading to the formation of the Queensland Baptist Association (Union) into which the German churches integrated in later years as full and valued members.

THE CHURCHES OF THE GERMAN BAPTIST CONFERENCE

THE BEGINNINGS

There were no ministers to labour among the German migrants of the 1860's, but the faithful testimony of lay men led to many conversions and baptisms, and to the formation of the churches at Zillman's waterholes (now Zillmere) and Logan. Support also came from some of the original German missionaries involved in the Gossner Mission's work at Zion's Hill, Nundah (German Station). These churches became extinct as people moved away from these areas to the scrub districts beyond Ipswich and on the Brisbane River which were then opening up for settlement.

Baptists may have been in present in the early 1860s at Normanby Reserve in the Harrisville/Mutdapilly area. Under the leadership of Mr. Schneider, their witness had become quite strong by 1867 and in 1871, a church was constituted. Previous to this, links were maintained with the Ipswich Church which was the centre for the first Baptist Association in Queensland, formed in 1870. Some of the settlers had moved further on to settle in the Coleyville Gap/Mt Walker area where a building was erected in 1868. This was soon to be the main centre until the work at Engelsburg (Kalbar) took the lead after 1875. But by 1886, Mt Walker was being supplied by Kalbar, a task taken over by Boonah in 1921, and the work closed down in 1967, just one hundred years after the first witness began.

Meanwhile, others had turned north and founded a church in the Fernvale/Vernor district on the Brisbane River, near Lowood in 1869. H. Falkenhager who had been a leader of work at Zillmere and Logan was set apart by the Ipswich Church in 1871 to lead this ministry. It was relocated south of Lowood in the 1890s and then to Tarampa in 1926. In 1870, these three fellowships amounted to about 150 members. In 1874, the German churches had formed their own conference. Another thriving church was also formed at Marburg (or Rosewood Scrub) in 1871, but the witness which began at the same time on the south side of the scrub at Lanefield and later removed to the town of Rosewood was not of German origin. Membership of the German churches in 1905 was around 550.

MARBURG

The church at Marburg was established in 1871 and was led by C. Dahn, C. Lamprecht and C. Arndt. At first, it sought affiliation with Mt Walker, but in 1875 it transferred it links to the Brisbane River church to the north, with the approval of the German Baptist Conference. Membership which began at 14 climbed to 113 by 1877, helped along by the transfer of 19 members from Zillman's Waterhole assembly near Brisbane. Also, during this tine, several families from Minden were associated with the Marburg church, prior to the establishment of their own fellowship. In 1879, Pastor Hermann Windolf, lately arrived from Germany, took pastoral charge of the two fellowships, as well as serving elsewhere as well. when his health failed, Pastor M. Bernoth arrived from Germany in 1885 to take leadership. His ministry was short, and he was succeeded by various lay men. Serious divisions plagued the church, to the extent even of the erection of a second building in the town, and links being set up with Ipswich.

The church joined with Lowood (Brisbane River), Minden and Blenheim in 1900 to call Rev. S. Blum, but ill—health cut his ministry short. Pastor Windolf returned in 1904 to lead the church until 1909. His successor, Pastor Imke was unable to find a house at Marburg, so arrangements were made for him to live in the vacant Minden manse, although a joint pastoral arrangement (to include Lowood as well) was rejected as unworkable. After 1914, Marburg church was linked in a joint pastorate with Lanefield (now Rosewood) church to the south under English pastors arranged through the Baptist Union of Queensland. In this way the Marburg church came under strong English influence from a comparatively early date, but it still retained its contacts with the German churches.

MINDEN

Minden Church undergoing alterations 1907

Baptist work first began in the Minden area, north-west of Ipswich in the late 1870's. Prior to this, Baptist families travelled down to Marburg (or Rosewood Scrub, as the area was then known) where a church had been established as early as 1871. But in 1884 a church fellowship was established at Minden and a year later Mr. Wilhelm Truloff donated an acre of land for a building and a cemetery. The church was opened in May with a large celebration which was customary, including a 'love feast' and a long revival meeting. The building has been renovated and modified over the years from 1907 until 1960 and a hall was erected in 1969.

No full-time pastor was appointed for some time, but Mr. J. Schultz and August Schmidt were devoted lay-preachers and leaders. From quite early times, the church participated in the German Conference, whose meetings were occasionally held at Minden. However in 1900, Minden in partnership with Lowood, Marburg and Blenheim churches called Pastor S. Blum from USA. A manse was built at Minden (the present building renovated) and the new pastor preached week about at the four churches. Later Tent Hill also joined the group. His ministry was greatly appreciated.

After Pastor Blum's departure due to ill-health in 1903, the church was served by pastors of other German churches. From 1903, Minden and Lowood worked together under the leadership of Pastor Franz Orthner, also of USA. (Removal expenses were 35 pounds and the annual stipend 110 pounds!) when he resigned in 1910 after the sad death of his young wife (daughter of a local family) and baby, the treasurer also resigned because he said that there was no work for him to do now that there was no stipend to pay!

The church was without a full-time pastor again until 1919. By then some English services had been introduced and an approach was made to the Baptist Union for help in securing a pastor. Rev. C. Cronau was the first English pastor, again in a sharing arrangement with Lowood. Membership at this time was around 80. A long line of distinguished ministers served the two churches until in 1958 Marburg also joined in the group. In 1982, the Tarampa Church (Lowood had moved there in 1926) left the group to work entirely independently.

KALBAR (ENGELSBURG) AND BOONAH

When the German Baptist Church which had been established at Mt Walker/Coleyville in 1867 agreed to the formation of a new fellowship at Engelsburg (officially known as Kalbar from 1963) in 1875, it was making an historic move. The new church, which dates its independence from 22 August of that year, soon took over from the pioneer fellowship as the centre of Baptist witness in the area.

Kalbar church band c.1907-15. (Pr. Windolf back row man not wearing a hat)

The leader of the new work was Mr. J. Stibbe and before long, the first of many baptismal services was being held. Some of these services saw the baptism of scores of candidates. The first building was erected in 1877 when the membership was 32. This church was replaced in 1882 and enlarged in 1891. Another church was erected on a new site in 1907 which in turn was enlarged at various times. A completely new modern building was erected in 1965. Maximum membership was 292 in 1936.

In 1877, Pastor Carl Krueger was appointed leader but he stepped aside a few months later to make way for Pastor H. Windolf who was joint pastor of Engelsburg and Mt walker. But a short time later, Pastor Windolf moved to Marburg and Pastor Krueger took up the work again in 1886, remaining in office until 1918. Pastor Windolf later returned to be his assistant during some of this time.

Engelsburg became a member of the Baptist Association (Union) in 1884, but withdrew in 1899 until taking up membership again in 1918 when it had an English pastor for the first time and many of its distinctive German features were beginning to be less noticeable. Most obvious of all was the use of the English language in services.

ALL DAY PICNIC AND SUNDAY SCHOOL CONCERT.
FIRST BAPTIST CHURCH BOONAH.21- 4-1919.

All day picnic and Sunday School Concert Boonah 1919

There were several outstations, some of them quite flourishing causes, at various times: Siloam (1896-1951); Charlwood (1908-); Aratula (1922-1972); Roadvale (1947-1973) and Warrill View (1946-1965). Boonah Church which was established by Engelsburg in 1887 (first at nearby Dugandan) became a strong independent church, but it is now linked with Kalbar again.

LAIDLEY (BLENHEIM)

Baptist Manse – Blenheim c. 1910

Baptist work in this area began when the Hermann Jackwitz, Carl Mutzleburg and F. Kerwitz and their families arrived at Sandy Creek or Blenheim in 1882-84 and worshipped in each other's homes. Other families from nearby areas soon joined them to create a strong Baptist community. They were in membership with the churches at Lowood or Marburg, whose pastors visited periodically for the ministry of the word. In time, a permanent link was established with Lowood as a branch church. Meetings were also held at Deep Gully and Laidley Creek, and a visit would be made occasionally to Lowood itself for worship, especially for the communion services.

Blenheim Church Date unknown

With growth in numbers, a building was necessary. So in 1892, there took place the opening and dedication of a church on a site donated by Mr. Jackwitz. It was burned to the ground in 1899 and another building was erected elsewhere, which was enlarged and renovated at various times in later years.

In 1895, an approach was made to the German Conference for recognition of the fellowship as an independent church. Foundation membership was 48 with Carl Mutzelburg as leader. He carried out an extensive and fruitful pastoral ministry in addition to his farming for several years until Rev. S. Blum was called from USA in 1900.

He served the churches of Lowood, Minden, and Marburg as well as Blenheim. He also began work in the Ma Ma Creek area which resulted in the establishment of an independent church at Tent Hill in 1901. The branches at Deep Gully and Left Hand Branch transferred from Blenheim to the new work, but the Hatton Vale fellowship transferred from Minden to Blenheim at about the same time. Blenheim and Tent Hill churches now combined together to call Rev. O. E. Kruger from USA. He arrived in December 1901, serving until 1908, being succeeded by Rev. J. Heinrich (also of USA) whose ministry spanned the period up to 1931.

Although the members were mostly of German background, in 1907 two 'English' people, William and Lucinda Dart were baptised. Later several members of the Dart family entered the Baptist ministry. (Others who entered the ministry from this church were Rev. E. V. Keith and Rev. G. Litzow.) Occasional English services were held from 1916 and German services were discontinued officially in 1930. In the same year, the church terminated its membership in the German Conference and became a member of the Baptist Union. The first English pastor, Rev. U.K. Holmans was appointed in 1931, almost 50 years after the commencement of witness in the district.

The link with Tent Hill was severed in 1935 when a new work commenced in Gatton demanded the pastor's attention. Blenheim continued under the leadership of Rev. S. Newell (1935-47). His successor, Pastor A. Law, pioneered services in the town of Laidley (1948 onwards) where the response led to the purchase of land. Although a move to transfer the work to Laidley in 1951 did not materialize, under the leadership of Rev. D. A. Dunlop, in 1952 a hall was erected in which to conduct regular evening services. Eventually, in January 1954, the decision was made to relocate. The last service was held in Blenheim on January 24, and in September of that year, the present church in Laidley was opened. Extensive redevelopments have taken place since under the continuing ministry of Mr. Dunlop, including the establishment of an aged persons home in 1968.

TENT HILL

Nestling up close to the valleys and spurs of the Great Divide, Tent Hill church had a pre-history of twenty years until it was officially constituted on 3 September 1901 in an impressive service attended by representatives of the five other German Conference churches. Its first building was erected a year later and it lasted until 1951 when a new one was erected which was remodelled in 1977. Growth was quick - from a foundation membership of 55, it had risen to 126 on its third anniversary.

But the early years were tough yet satisfying as the settlers carved out an existence in the scrubs of Deep Gully, Left Hand Branch, Mt Sylvia and Ma Ma Creek. At the same time, they were faithful in their witness and fellowship travelling miles in difficult circumstances for worship and evangelism.

Pastoral oversight was provided by Pastor S. Blum who had come from USA to serve some of the other German churches (Blenheim, Lowood, Minden and Marburg). when Tent Hill was constituted, Pastor Otto Krueger was called from USA and took up his work as joint pastor of Tent Hill and Blenheim (where he lived) in 1902. He was succeeded in 1908 by another American German, Pastor J. Heinrich. It was not until the end of his ministry in 1930 that the first Queensland trained, English pastor was appointed in the person of Rev. U.K. Holmans. By this time, English had been in use for almost 15 years. In 1930, the church joined the Baptist Union of Queensland.

An important outreach of the church under the leadership of Pastor Holmans was the establishment in 1935 of work in Gatton. So fruitful was this ministry that Mr. Holmans became joint pastor of Tent Hill-Gatton, leaving Blenheim to call its own pastor. (The work was transferred to Laidley in 1954.) A similar move took place in 1978 when the Gatton Church asked for the join pastorate with Tent Hill to be terminated, both churches becoming independent. Tent Hill purchased a manse at the nearby town of Grantham, and found new avenues of service in the farming areas to the west and south.

THANKS Sincere thanks is expressed to all those who assisted in the Celebration, with extra thanks to Mr. Dick Scanlan, local convener, the pastor and members of Laidley Baptist Church for arrangements, and the representatives of each church who made up the steering committee. Thanks is also expressed to Mr. Glenn Roberts for his long-standing interest in and commitment to research on the German Baptist work and to Rev. John White for his contribution. Thanks is also expressed to Jan Mengel for assistance with the production of this Newsletter and to Andrew Savage for preparing the display map.

The historical notes printed in this issue have been based upon the printed histories of the churches, and the following:

Queensland Baptist Jubilee Volume 1905
A Fellowship of Service by Rev. J.E. White (1977)
A History of the German Baptist Churches, by Rev. P.G. Bryant (1982)

6. THE CONFERENCE OF GERMAN BAPTISTS IN SOUTH-EAST QUEENSLAND
by Glenn Roberts

Sometime in 1874, two church assemblies comprising a unique ethnic minority, German migrants of Baptist persuasion, called after their place names Brisbane River and Mount Walker, festively met and formed an association. Both had been formed separately about ten years previously as these pioneering migrants moved outwards from Brisbane. The 'South Queensland German Baptist Society' was to grow to over three times its size and last for about sixty years, though undergoing several reforms and many setbacks.

They were brought together by powerful forces - isolation and a sense of minority and, most important of all, spiritual hunger. There was an understandable urge for fellowship with those of common mind and origin amongst the settlers in the new land, which was regarded also as a mission field by many of them. Another factor was language - it would have been of little help to meet with English-speaking Baptists based at the nearest town, Ipswich and elsewhere.

Their feelings were often expressed in reports sent back to Germany for printing in missionary magazines. The earliest known report of this kind was from Brother Heinrich Moller of Normanby Reserve (dated 6 July 1871) to the founder of the German Baptist movement, Rev. J. G. Oncken. He said, 'while our assembly arose about four years ago from five members, the number now amounts to 60.' He also spoke of a 'richly blessed Pentecost with a Lovefeast' at which 25 people were converted. Pastor H. Windolf wrote later about the arrival of the first Baptists in June 1865, of the first converts in the Nundah area and of outreach to Normanby Station. Other reports referred to the opening of a chapel at Mt. Walker in October 1871 when friends from many districts gathered for fellowship, and also of a thriving work on the Brisbane River near Lowood.

These early foundations of the Conference were extended in 1875 when a third member joined the group, the church at Fassifern Scrub (Kalbar or Engelsburg). The next to join was 'Rosewood Scrub' (Marburg) in 1876. It had gained some members by transfer from Mt Walker and was 'the most important German settlement in which a few thousand Germans are said to live - to use Pastor Windolf's words. They were also joined by some from the Zillmere area.

A report from Mt Walker dated 9 April 1877 (the same year as the Baptist Union of Queensland was being commenced) said 'six churches have now arisen, with 300 members and five chapels." Only 31 of these were believers on arrival from Germany! At a meeting in Marburg, 200 were present at an Easter love-feast, and 72 pounds was sent to Germany towards procuring a preacher. It was through drawing together (Zusammenziehen) newly migrated brethren and growth of new converts' that isolation was overcome and solidarity achieved.

A major need of the conference churches was met in 1878 when the long-awaited trained pastor arrived from Germany in the person of Pastor Hermann Windolf. A joyful description of this event was reported in the missionary magazine. It was also noted that a second worker would soon be required. However, the new arrangements resulted in a breakdown in the fledgling conference because of personal and policy differences between Pastor Windolf and the lay leaders at Fassifern.

Minor meetings were still convened between the churches in the succeeding years, as is indicated by scattered reports in German periodicals. For example, there was a new Bethel chapel at Marburg to which members from Brisbane River, Brisbane and even the Logan were invited. In September 1881, a small conference met at Marburg including members from Zillman's Waterholes.

'Peace between Marburg, FASSIFERN and Mt Walker" was announced in Windolf's handwritten minutes following a meeting of reconciliation at Fassifern on 12 July 1882. There had also developed two churches at Brisbane River ('on the river' and "in the scrub') and these were united in March 1884. Two months later, a motion at Marburg called for the unification of Brisbane River, Rosewood (Marburg), Mt Walker and Fassifern Assemblies! But even this was not to be, as further difficulties resulted in divisions even in Marburg itself.

The Fassifern church and Pastor Windolf in 1887 exhorted the members to reconciliation and to consider uniting with the English Baptists. However, there was little progress for it was reported that there were two German groups at Marburg, three around Brisbane River and also Mt walker, but Engelsburg and Minden were in the English Association.

A major reform of the German Conference must have taken place around 1889 although the records are missing until 1890. But a meeting at Engelsburg in October 1891 is referred to as the 'third' such meeting, and the number of churches was now six. The next two years were quite stable with five churches totalling over 400 members. Blenheim came into the conference in 1895, but Engelsburg withdrew again and the following year, so did Mt Walker. Records of some later conferences have come to light in recent times, enabling a further documentation of the life of the Conference.

The turn of the century meant a conference turning point as new fellowship - ... Tent Hill - joined and new trained pastor arrived from America, Rev. Samuel Blum. The reform he brought about led to a total revival in conference life, even drawing Engelsburg back into the circle in a meeting in 1901. By then Minden had reached 50 members under a lay-leader A. Schmidt, Lowood/Fernvale had 80 under U. Litzow and Marburg had 35 under U. Meissner.

An outward change in the conference was its new placing in the year - generally at Easter time, and a new constitution was adopted. (This can be found printed in the official history of Laidley Church.) From 1902 to 1913, the venues rotated twice in this pattern: Engelsburg, Blenheim, Minden, Marburg, Tent Hill and Lowood. Outstations included Kingaroy, Esk and Redland Bay. A copy of the proceedings from 1904 was found in Hamburg 80 years later. It had been called 'Conference of Peace in the King's Vale', opening at 7pm Thursday 24 March, and containing four sessions. Reports showed that they had 319 Sunday School children, 59 newly baptised believers and total offerings had come to 489 pounds. Topics discussed included the keeping of the Sabbath, support for the Mayurbhanj Mission in India where Miss Martha Huth served, and the distribution of Christian tracts. On other occasions, they debated military service, involvement in Government positions and the Christian attitude to dancing and drinking. Discipline on church members was usually quite strong.

Engelsburg (Kalbar) c. 1910

Before the war broke out in 1914, the conference met at Engelsburg, soon to have its name changed to Kalbar. By then, Lowood had an outstation called Coal Creek with 92 members and Minden with Kingaroy had 76; Marburg with its outstations reached 110.

Minden 1907

By 1927, the Baptist Union of Queensland gave the statistics of the German churches individually and not as a group which suggests that the Conference had ceased to function by then, though some evidence indicates that Tent Hill church belonged to it until 1930. As late as 1932, the German language was still being used occasionally in some churches. But it seems generally that the Conference declined with the use of the language and thus this body became a thing of the past, preserved mainly in documents that have only partly been translated and in the minds of its participants. As long as its members remained ethnically isolated, it served its purpose well.

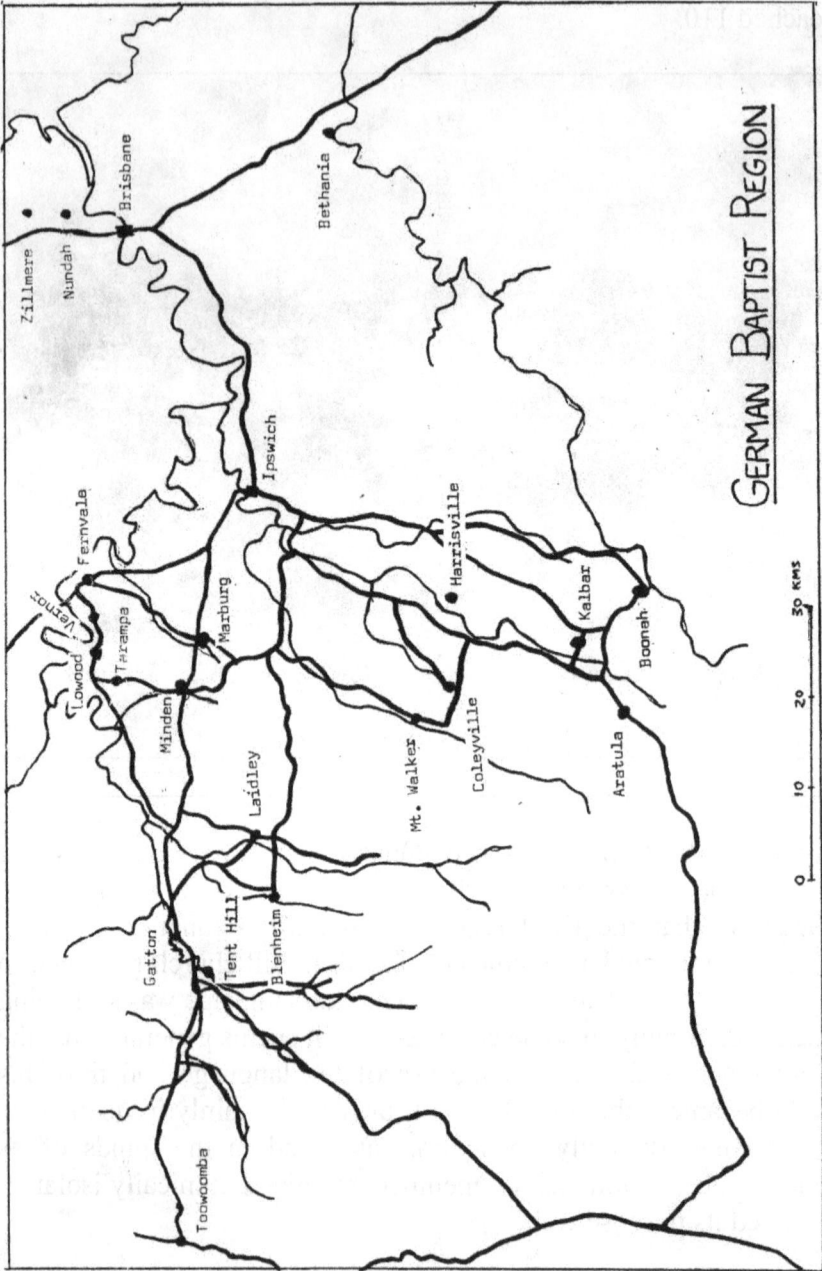

GERMAN BAPTIST REGION

SOURCE OF IMAGES

Image	Source
Cover	State Library of Queensland
Braunschweig	Wikipedia
Johann Gerhard Oncken	Wikipedia
Embarkation Record	Archive BallinStadt Emigration Museum Hamburg, Germany
Embarcation Hamburg	Archive BallinStadt Emigration Museum Hamburg, Germany
Hamburg Harbour 1875	Through Scandinavian Eyes - a History of Colonial Queensland. http://orsted-jensen.weebly.com/scandinavians-in-pre-1914-australia.html
West India Docks	www.eastlondonpostcard.co.uk
The Gauntlet clipper ship	State Library of Queensland
The Sussex	Methin Heritage, Methil Tugs http://www.methilheritage.org.uk/content/pages/methil-docks/methil-tugs.php
Plymouth Harbour	Plymouth History Appreciation Society Facebook page
Portland Harbour	https://susanhogben.wordpress.com/category/portland-roads/
Lebensweker	Phisick – Antique medical and surgical http://phisick.com/item/baunscheidts-lebenswecker-ebony/
Hamilton 1878	State Library of Queensland
Clearing Fassifern Scrub	State Library of Queensland
German farming family in Fassifern Valley	State Library of Queensland
German Baptist Ministers	State Library of Queensland

German Settlers, Rosewood Scrub	State Library of Queensland
Pastor Bernoth	South Queensland Adventist Heritage http://sqheritage.adventist.org.au/history
Marburg Baptist Church 1905	State Library of Queensland
Kalbar Baptist Church Band	State Library of Queensland
Herman Windolf in Old Age	Selwyn Windolf
Baptist Manse Blenheim	State Library of Queensland
Englesburg 1910	State Library of Queensland
Minden 1907	State Library of Queensland
Map	Baptist Heritage Queensland
Other Baptist Churches	Baptist Heritage Queensland

REFERENCES

-------- The Gauntlet Clipper Ship in *London Illustrated News*, (Aug 27, 1853, 164).

Burrage, Henry S. *Baptist Hymn Writers And Their Hymns.* (Portland: Brown Thurston & Company, 1888)

Schauffler, William G. *Autobiobraphy of William G Schauffler* (New York: Anson D.F, Randolf and Company, 1887)

Roberts, Glenn, *The Life, Writings And Work Of Hermann Windolf 1846-1922* (1986, no other publication data available).

Roberts, Glenn. The Conference Of German Baptists In South-East Queensland In *Baptist Historical Society of Queensland Newsletter* (No 5 July 1986).

White, John. The Beginnings Of The German Baptist Witness in *Baptist Historical Society of Queensland Newsletter* (No 5 July 1986).

Windolf, Herman, The voyage of Brother H. Windolf in *Der Pilgor.* (1878. 6ff).

Windolf, Herman, Memoir Pages on the Baptist Mission among the Germans in Queensland in Australia in *The Wahrheitszeuge.* Translated by Glenn Roberts. (1879).

INTERNET SITES

-------- Johann Gerhard Oncken in Wikipedia http://en.wikipedia.org/wiki/ Johann_Gerhard_Oncken. Date accessed 20 September, 2014

-------- Phisick – Antique medical and surgical http://phisick.com /item/baunscheidts-lebenswecker-ebony/ Date accessed September 20, 2014

----------- BallinStadt Emigration Museum http://english.hamburg. de/ballinstadt/. Date Accessed September 20, 1914.

-------- the Doric Columns – the Clipper Ships http://mcjazz.f2s.com/Clippers.htm. Date accessed September 29, 2014.

-------- .South Queensland Adventist Heritage http://sqheritage. adventist.org.au/history. Date accessed 29 September 2014.

Payne, Ernest A. Julius Kobner and the German Baptists in *The Baptist Quarterly* UD 389. http://www.biblicalstudies.org.uk/pdf/ bq/04-8_380.pdf. Date accessed 29 September 2014.

Langbridge, Catherine, Robert Sloan and Regina Ganter. *German Missionaries in Australia* Griffith University http://missionaries.griffith.edu.au/qld-mission/zion-hill-mission-1838-1848. Date accessed 27 September 2014.

Maxfield, Charles A. *The Creation of the United Church of Christ in South Dakota.* Dec. 1989. http://www.maxfieldbooks.com/ UCCinND.html#S2d. Date accessed Oct 27, 2014.

New Apostolic Hymnal. http://www.nak-gesangbuch.de/index. php?l=en. Date accessed 6 October, 2014.

Windolf, Herman. Report of Hamburg Ministry in *Sword and Trowel* June 1865. http://www.godrules.net/library/spurgeon/ NEW9spurgeon_a9.htm. Date accessed 22 October 2014.

ABOUT THE EDITOR

Edgar (Ted) Stubbersfield grew up in the small town of Gatton in Queensland, Australia in the 50's. It was a good time to be young. Life was simple, relatively safe and faith in God was taken for granted. After being thrown out of school in 1965 he started an apprenticeship as a motor mechanic, something he was ill suited to. In 1970, Ted went on an extended trip overseas and was confronted by the Christian gospel in many countries and saw for the first time that there was a God who was alive. That year he met with Jesus in a Damascus road type experience.

Ministry seemed to be the logical call on his life and he trained initially with the Church of Christ and then in the UK with the Elim Pentecostal Church but found himself most at home with a remarkable group of Grace Baptists. The Lord had mercy on His church and Ted went back to the family business, a sawmill. He kept his interest in Christian faith, living and doctrine by studying by correspondence and by writing.

Ted has a number of other publications but in a very different field, weather exposed timber structures. He is currently working as a consultant in this field.

He completed a Master of Theology in Applied Theology in 2011 through the University of Wales.

www.ingramcontent.com/pod-product-compliance
Lightning Source LLC
Chambersburg PA
CBHW060134050426
42448CB00010B/2127